CAMPING
JOURNAL

NAME: _____

PHONE: _____

Camping Camper

JOURNALS

Campground: Dates:

Location:_____

Travel to Campground: *Miles:*_____ *Time:*_____ *Cost:*_____

Weather : ☀️ ☐ ⛅ ☐ ☁️ ☐ 🌧️ ☐ ⛈️ ☐ ❄️ ☐

Campground Information

Name:_____

Address:_____

Phone:_____

Site#:_____ Site for next time:_____

Cost:_____ $ ☐ Day ☐ Week ☐ Month

GPS:_____

Rating: ★☆☆☆☆☆☆☆☆☆

Water pressure ★☆☆☆☆ Location ★☆☆☆☆

Cleanliness ★☆☆☆☆ Site size ★☆☆☆☆

Restrooms ★☆☆☆☆ Noise ★☆☆☆☆

Amenities:

☐ easy access   ☐ back-in   ☐ pull-through
☐ water   ☐ pet friendly ☐ laundry
☐ paved   ☐ sewer   ☐ electricity
☐ 15 amp   ☐ 30 amp   ☐ 50 amp
☐ shade   ☐ pool   ☐ restrooms
☐ store   ☐ picnic table ☐ fire ring
☐ firewood   ☐ tv   ☐ wifi
☐ security   ☐ ice   ☐ cafe

Activities:

☐ fishing   ☐ hiking   ☐ canoeing
☐ lake   ☐ river   ☐ hot tub
☐ fitness   ☐ bike   ☐ boat
☐ shuffleboard   ☐ pickleball ☐ golf

Camped with:_____

_____

_____

Places visited:_____

_____

_____

Visit/do next time:_____

_____

_____

Most memorable event:

_____

_____

Most fun things:

_____

_____

_____

Notes:

_____

_____

_____

_____

_____

Drawing or favorite photo:

Campground: _____ Dates: _____

Location: _____

Travel to Campground: *Miles:* _____ *Time:* _____ *Cost:* _____

Weather : ☀️ ⛅ ☁️ 🌧️ ⛈️ ❄️
☐ ☐ ☐ ☐ ☐ ☐

Campground Information

Name: _____

Address: _____

Phone: _____

Site#: _____ Site for next time: _____

Cost: _____ $ ☐ Day ☐Week ☐Month

GPS: _____

Rating: ★☆☆☆☆☆☆☆☆☆

Water pressure ★☆☆☆☆ Location ★☆☆☆☆

Cleanliness ★☆☆☆☆ Site size ★☆☆☆☆

Restrooms ★☆☆☆☆ Noise ★☆☆☆☆

Amenities:

☐ easy access ☐ back-in   ☐ pull-through
☐ water   ☐ pet friendly ☐ laundry
☐ paved   ☐ sewer   ☐ electricity
☐ 15 amp   ☐ 30 amp   ☐ 50 amp
☐ shade   ☐ pool   ☐ restrooms
☐ store   ☐ picnic table ☐ fire ring
☐ firewood   ☐ tv   ☐ wifi
☐ security   ☐ ice   ☐ cafe

Activities:

☐ fishing   ☐ hiking   ☐ canoeing
☐ lake   ☐ river   ☐ hot tub
☐ fitness   ☐ bike   ☐ boat
☐ shuffleboard ☐ pickleball   ☐ golf

Camped with: _____

_____

_____

Places visited: _____

_____

_____

Visit/do next time: _____

_____

_____

Most memorable event:_____
_____

Most fun things:_____
_____
_____
_____

Notes:_____
_____
_____
_____
_____

Drawing or favorite photo:

Campground: Dates:

Location:_____

Travel to Campground: *Miles:* _____ *Time:* _____ *Cost:* _____

Weather : ☐ ☐ ☐ ☐ ☐ ☐

Campground Information

Name:_____

Address:_____

Phone:_____

Site#:_____ Site for next time:_____

Cost:_____ $ ☐ Day ☐Week ☐Month

GPS:_____

Rating: ★☆☆☆☆☆☆☆☆☆

Water pressure ★☆☆☆☆ Location ★☆☆☆☆

Cleanliness ★☆☆☆☆ Site size ★☆☆☆☆

Restrooms ★☆☆☆☆ Noise ★☆☆☆☆

Amenities:

☐ easy access   ☐ back-in   ☐ pull-through
☐ water   ☐ pet friendly   ☐ laundry
☐ paved   ☐ sewer   ☐ electricity
☐ 15 amp   ☐ 30 amp   ☐ 50 amp
☐ shade   ☐ pool   ☐ restrooms
☐ store   ☐ picnic table   ☐ fire ring
☐ firewood   ☐ tv   ☐ wifi
☐ security   ☐ ice   ☐ cafe

Activities:

☐ fishing   ☐ hiking   ☐ canoeing
☐ lake   ☐ river   ☐ hot tub
☐ fitness   ☐ bike   ☐ boat
☐ shuffleboard   ☐ pickleball   ☐ golf

Camped with:_____

_____

_____

Places visited:_____

_____

_____

Visit/do next time:_____

_____

_____

Most memorable event:

Most fun things:

Notes:

Drawing or favorite photo:

Campground: _____ **Dates:** _____

Location: _____

Travel to Campground: *Miles:* _____ *Time:* _____ *Cost:* _____

Weather : ☀ ⛅ ☁ 🌧 ⛈ ❄

☐ ☐ ☐ ☐ ☐ ☐

Campground Information

Name: _____

Address: _____

Phone: _____

Site#: _____ **Site for next time:** _____

Cost: _____ $ ☐ Day ☐ Week ☐ Month

GPS: _____

Rating: ★☆☆☆☆☆☆☆☆☆

Water pressure ★☆☆☆☆ **Location** ★☆☆☆☆

Cleanliness ★☆☆☆☆ **Site size** ★☆☆☆☆

Restrooms ★☆☆☆☆ **Noise** ★☆☆☆☆

Amenities:

☐ easy access	☐ back-in	☐ pull-through
☐ water	☐ pet friendly	☐ laundry
☐ paved	☐ sewer	☐ electricity
☐ 15 amp	☐ 30 amp	☐ 50 amp
☐ shade	☐ pool	☐ restrooms
☐ store	☐ picnic table	☐ fire ring
☐ firewood	☐ tv	☐ wifi
☐ security	☐ ice	☐ cafe

Activities:

☐ fishing	☐ hiking	☐ canoeing
☐ lake	☐ river	☐ hot tub
☐ fitness	☐ bike	☐ boat
☐ shuffleboard	☐ pickleball	☐ golf

Camped with: _____

_____

Places visited: _____

_____

Visit/do next time: _____

_____

Most memorable event:

Most fun things:

Notes:

Drawing or favorite photo:

Campground: _____ **Dates:** _____

Location:_____

Travel to Campground: *Miles:* _____ *Time:* _____ *Cost:* _____

Weather : ☐ ☐ ☐ ☐ ☐ ☐

Campground Information

Name:_____

Address:_____

Phone:_____

Site#:_____ Site for next time:_____

Cost:_____ $ ☐ Day ☐Week ☐Month

GPS:_____

Rating: ★☆☆☆☆☆☆☆☆☆

Water pressure ★☆☆☆☆ Location ★☆☆☆☆

Cleanliness ★☆☆☆☆ Site size ★☆☆☆☆

Restrooms ★☆☆☆☆ Noise ★☆☆☆☆

Amenities:

☐ easy access   ☐ back-in   ☐ pull-through
☐ water   ☐ pet friendly   ☐ laundry
☐ paved   ☐ sewer   ☐ electricity
☐ 15 amp   ☐ 30 amp   ☐ 50 amp
☐ shade   ☐ pool   ☐ restrooms
☐ store   ☐ picnic table   ☐ fire ring
☐ firewood   ☐ tv   ☐ wifi
☐ security   ☐ ice   ☐ cafe

Activities:

☐ fishing   ☐ hiking   ☐ canoeing
☐ lake   ☐ river   ☐ hot tub
☐ fitness   ☐ bike   ☐ boat
☐ shuffleboard   ☐ pickleball   ☐ golf

Camped with:_____

_____

_____

Places visited:_____

_____

Visit/do next time:_____

_____

_____

Most memorable event:_____

_____

Most fun things:_____

_____

_____

_____

Notes:_____

_____

_____

_____

_____

Drawing or favorite photo:

Campground: **Dates:**

Location: _____

Travel to Campground: *Miles:* _____ *Time:* _____ *Cost:* _____

Weather : ☀ ☐   🌤 ☐   ☁ ☐   🌧 ☐   ⛈ ☐   ❄ ☐

Campground Information

Name: _____

Address: _____

Phone: _____

Site#: _____ Site for next time: _____

Cost: _____ $ ☐ Day ☐ Week ☐ Month

GPS: _____

Rating: ★☆☆☆☆☆☆☆☆☆

Water pressure ★☆☆☆☆ **Location** ★☆☆☆☆

Cleanliness ★☆☆☆☆ **Site size** ★☆☆☆☆

Restrooms ★☆☆☆☆ **Noise** ★☆☆☆☆

Amenities:

☐ easy access ☐ back-in ☐ pull-through
☐ water ☐ pet friendly ☐ laundry
☐ paved ☐ sewer ☐ electricity
☐ 15 amp ☐ 30 amp ☐ 50 amp
☐ shade ☐ pool ☐ restrooms
☐ store ☐ picnic table ☐ fire ring
☐ firewood ☐ tv ☐ wifi
☐ security ☐ ice ☐ cafe

Activities:

☐ fishing ☐ hiking ☐ canoeing
☐ lake ☐ river ☐ hot tub
☐ fitness ☐ bike ☐ boat
☐ shuffleboard ☐ pickleball ☐ golf

Camped with: _____

_____

_____

Places visited: _____

_____

_____

Visit/do next time: _____

_____

_____

Most memorable event:

Most fun things:

Notes:

Drawing or favorite photo:

Campground: Dates:

Location:_____

Travel to Campground: *Miles:*_____ *Time:*_____ *Cost:*_____

Weather : ☀️ ☐   ⛅ ☐   ☁️ ☐   🌧️ ☐   ⛈️ ☐   ❄️ ☐

Campground Information

Name:_____

Address:_____

Phone:_____

Site#:_____ Site for next time:_____

Cost:_____ $ ☐ Day ☐Week ☐Month

GPS:_____

Rating: ★☆☆☆☆☆☆☆☆☆

Water pressure ★☆☆☆☆☆ Location ★☆☆☆☆☆

Cleanliness ★☆☆☆☆☆ Site size ★☆☆☆☆☆

Restrooms ★☆☆☆☆☆ Noise ★☆☆☆☆☆

Amenities:

☐ easy access	☐ back-in	☐ pull-through
☐ water	☐ pet friendly	☐ laundry
☐ paved	☐ sewer	☐ electricity
☐ 15 amp	☐ 30 amp	☐ 50 amp
☐ shade	☐ pool	☐ restrooms
☐ store	☐ picnic table	☐ fire ring
☐ firewood	☐ tv	☐ wifi
☐ security	☐ ice	☐ cafe

Activities:

☐ fishing	☐ hiking	☐ canoeing
☐ lake	☐ river	☐ hot tub
☐ fitness	☐ bike	☐ boat
☐ shuffleboard	☐ pickleball	☐ golf

Camped with:_____

_____

_____

Places visited:_____

_____

_____

Visit/do next time:_____

_____

_____

Most memorable event:_____

_____

Most fun things:_____

_____

_____

Notes:_____

_____

_____

_____

_____

Drawing or favorite photo:

Campground: Dates:

Location:_____

Travel to Campground: *Miles:* _____ *Time:* _____ *Cost:* _____

Weather : ☀️ ⛅ ☁️ 🌧️ ⛈️ ❄️
☐   ☐   ☐   ☐   ☐   ☐

Campground Information

Name:_____

Address:_____

Phone:_____

Site#:_____ Site for next time:_____

Cost:_____ $ ☐ Day ☐Week ☐Month

GPS:_____

Rating: ★☆☆☆☆☆☆☆☆☆

Water pressure ★☆☆☆☆☆ **Location** ★☆☆☆☆☆

Cleanliness ★☆☆☆☆☆ **Site size** ★☆☆☆☆☆

Restrooms ★☆☆☆☆☆ **Noise** ★☆☆☆☆☆

Amenities:

☐ easy access   ☐ back-in   ☐ pull-through
☐ water   ☐ pet friendly   ☐ laundry
☐ paved   ☐ sewer   ☐ electricity
☐ 15 amp   ☐ 30 amp   ☐ 50 amp
☐ shade   ☐ pool   ☐ restrooms
☐ store   ☐ picnic table   ☐ fire ring
☐ firewood   ☐ tv   ☐ wifi
☐ security   ☐ ice   ☐ cafe

Activities:

☐ fishing   ☐ hiking   ☐ canoeing
☐ lake   ☐ river   ☐ hot tub
☐ fitness   ☐ bike   ☐ boat
☐ shuffleboard   ☐ pickleball   ☐ golf

Camped with:_____

_____

Places visited:_____

_____

Visit/do next time:_____

_____

Most memorable event: _____

_____
_____

Most fun things: _____

_____
_____
_____

Notes: _____

_____
_____
_____
_____

Drawing or favorite photo:

Campground: Dates:

Location:_____

Travel to Campground: *Miles:* _____ *Time:* _____ *Cost:* _____

Weather : ☐ ☐ ☐ ☐ ☐ ☐

Campground Information

Name:_____

Address:_____

Phone:_____

Site#:_____ Site for next time:_____

Cost:_____ $ ☐ Day ☐Week ☐Month

GPS:_____

Rating: ★☆☆☆☆☆☆☆☆☆

Water pressure ★☆☆☆☆ Location ★☆☆☆☆

Cleanliness ★☆☆☆☆ Site size ★☆☆☆☆

Restrooms ★☆☆☆☆ Noise ★☆☆☆☆

Amenities:

☐ easy access ☐ back-in ☐ pull-through
☐ water ☐ pet friendly ☐ laundry
☐ paved ☐ sewer ☐ electricity
☐ 15 amp ☐ 30 amp ☐ 50 amp
☐ shade ☐ pool ☐ restrooms
☐ store ☐ picnic table ☐ fire ring
☐ firewood ☐ tv ☐ wifi
☐ security ☐ ice ☐ cafe

Activities:

☐ fishing ☐ hiking ☐ canoeing
☐ lake ☐ river ☐ hot tub
☐ fitness ☐ bike ☐ boat
☐ shuffleboard ☐ pickleball ☐ golf

Camped with:_____

_____

Places visited:_____

_____

Visit/do next time:_____

_____

Most memorable event:_____

_____

Most fun things:_____

_____

_____

Notes:_____

_____

_____

_____

_____

Drawing or favorite photo:

Campground: _____ **Dates:** _____

Location: _____

Travel to Campground: *Miles:* _____ *Time:* _____ *Cost:* _____

Weather : ☀️ ☐ ⛅ ☐ ☁️ ☐ 🌧️ ☐ ⛈️ ☐ ❄️ ☐

Campground Information

Name: _____

Address: _____

Phone: _____

Site#: _____ **Site for next time:** _____

Cost: _____ $ ☐ Day ☐ Week ☐ Month

GPS: _____

Rating: ★☆☆☆☆☆☆☆☆☆

Water pressure ★☆☆☆☆ **Location** ★☆☆☆☆

Cleanliness ★☆☆☆☆ **Site size** ★☆☆☆☆

Restrooms ★☆☆☆☆ **Noise** ★☆☆☆☆

Amenities:

☐ easy access ☐ back-in ☐ pull-through
☐ water ☐ pet friendly ☐ laundry
☐ paved ☐ sewer ☐ electricity
☐ 15 amp ☐ 30 amp ☐ 50 amp
☐ shade ☐ pool ☐ restrooms
☐ store ☐ picnic table ☐ fire ring
☐ firewood ☐ tv ☐ wifi
☐ security ☐ ice ☐ cafe

Activities:

☐ fishing ☐ hiking ☐ canoeing
☐ lake ☐ river ☐ hot tub
☐ fitness ☐ bike ☐ boat
☐ shuffleboard ☐ pickleball ☐ golf

Camped with: _____

_____

_____

Places visited: _____

_____

_____

Visit/do next time: _____

_____

_____

Most memorable event:_____

_____

Most fun things:_____

_____

_____

_____

Notes:_____

_____

_____

_____

_____

Drawing or favorite photo:

Campground: _____ **Dates:** _____

Location: _____

Travel to Campground: *Miles:* _____ *Time:* _____ *Cost:* _____

Weather : ☀️ ⛅ ☁️ 🌧️ ⛈️ ❄️

☐ ☐ ☐ ☐ ☐ ☐

Campground Information

Name: _____

Address: _____

Phone: _____

Site#: _____ **Site for next time:** _____

Cost: _____ $ ☐ Day ☐ Week ☐ Month

GPS: _____

Rating: ★☆☆☆☆☆☆☆☆☆

Water pressure ★☆☆☆☆☆ **Location** ★☆☆☆☆☆

Cleanliness ★☆☆☆☆☆ **Site size** ★☆☆☆☆☆

Restrooms ★☆☆☆☆☆ **Noise** ★☆☆☆☆☆

Amenities:

☐ easy access	☐ back-in	☐ pull-through
☐ water	☐ pet friendly	☐ laundry
☐ paved	☐ sewer	☐ electricity
☐ 15 amp	☐ 30 amp	☐ 50 amp
☐ shade	☐ pool	☐ restrooms
☐ store	☐ picnic table	☐ fire ring
☐ firewood	☐ tv	☐ wifi
☐ security	☐ ice	☐ cafe

Activities:

☐ fishing	☐ hiking	☐ canoeing
☐ lake	☐ river	☐ hot tub
☐ fitness	☐ bike	☐ boat
☐ shuffleboard	☐ pickleball	☐ golf

Camped with: _____

_____

Places visited: _____

_____

Visit/do next time: _____

_____

Most memorable event:

Most fun things:

Notes:

Drawing or favorite photo:

Campground: _____ **Dates:** _____

Location: _____

Travel to Campground: *Miles:* _____ *Time:* _____ *Cost:* _____

Weather : ☀️ ⛅ ☁️ 🌧️ ⛈️ ❄️
　　　　　　 ⬜　⬜　⬜　⬜　⬜　⬜

Campground Information

Name: _____

Address: _____

Phone: _____

Site#: _____ Site for next time: _____

Cost: _____ $ ☐ Day ☐ Week ☐ Month

GPS: _____

Rating: ★☆☆☆☆☆☆☆☆☆

Water pressure ★☆☆☆☆☆ Location ★☆☆☆☆☆

Cleanliness ★☆☆☆☆☆ Site size ★☆☆☆☆☆

Restrooms ★☆☆☆☆☆ Noise ★☆☆☆☆☆

Amenities:

☐ easy access	☐ back-in	☐ pull-through
☐ water	☐ pet friendly	☐ laundry
☐ paved	☐ sewer	☐ electricity
☐ 15 amp	☐ 30 amp	☐ 50 amp
☐ shade	☐ pool	☐ restrooms
☐ store	☐ picnic table	☐ fire ring
☐ firewood	☐ tv	☐ wifi
☐ security	☐ ice	☐ cafe

Activities:

☐ fishing	☐ hiking	☐ canoeing
☐ lake	☐ river	☐ hot tub
☐ fitness	☐ bike	☐ boat
☐ shuffleboard	☐ pickleball	☐ golf

Camped with: _____

_____

Places visited: _____

_____

Visit/do next time: _____

_____

Most memorable event:

Most fun things:

Notes:

Drawing or favorite photo:

Campground: _____ Dates: _____

Location: _____

Travel to Campground: *Miles:* _____ *Time:* _____ *Cost:* _____

Weather : ☀️ 🌤️ ☁️ 🌧️ ⛈️ ❄️
☐ ☐ ☐ ☐ ☐ ☐

Campground Information

Name: _____

Address: _____

Phone: _____

Site#: _____ Site for next time: _____

Cost: _____ $ ☐ Day ☐Week ☐Month

GPS: _____

Rating: ★☆☆☆☆☆☆☆☆☆

Water pressure ★☆☆☆☆☆ **Location** ★☆☆☆☆☆

Cleanliness ★☆☆☆☆☆ **Site size** ★☆☆☆☆☆

Restrooms ★☆☆☆☆☆ **Noise** ★☆☆☆☆☆

Amenities:

☐ easy access ☐ back-in ☐ pull-through
☐ water ☐ pet friendly ☐ laundry
☐ paved ☐ sewer ☐ electricity
☐ 15 amp ☐ 30 amp ☐ 50 amp
☐ shade ☐ pool ☐ restrooms
☐ store ☐ picnic table ☐ fire ring
☐ firewood ☐ tv ☐ wifi
☐ security ☐ ice ☐ cafe

Activities:

☐ fishing ☐ hiking ☐ canoeing
☐ lake ☐ river ☐ hot tub
☐ fitness ☐ bike ☐ boat
☐ shuffleboard ☐ pickleball ☐ golf

Camped with: _____
_____
_____

Places visited: _____
_____
_____

Visit/do next time: _____
_____
_____

Most memorable event:

Most fun things:

Notes:

Drawing or favorite photo:

Campground: _____ **Dates:** _____

Location: _____

Travel to Campground: *Miles:* _____ *Time:* _____ *Cost:* _____

Weather : ☐ ☐ ☐ ☐ ☐ ☐

Campground Information

Name: _____

Address: _____

Phone: _____

Site#: _____ **Site for next time:** _____

Cost: _____ $ ☐ Day ☐ Week ☐ Month

GPS: _____

Rating: ★☆☆☆☆☆☆☆☆☆

Water pressure ★☆☆☆☆ **Location** ★☆☆☆☆

Cleanliness ★☆☆☆☆ **Site size** ★☆☆☆☆

Restrooms ★☆☆☆☆ **Noise** ★☆☆☆☆

Amenities:

☐ easy access ☐ back-in ☐ pull-through
☐ water ☐ pet friendly ☐ laundry
☐ paved ☐ sewer ☐ electricity
☐ 15 amp ☐ 30 amp ☐ 50 amp
☐ shade ☐ pool ☐ restrooms
☐ store ☐ picnic table ☐ fire ring
☐ firewood ☐ tv ☐ wifi
☐ security ☐ ice ☐ cafe

Activities:

☐ fishing ☐ hiking ☐ canoeing
☐ lake ☐ river ☐ hot tub
☐ fitness ☐ bike ☐ boat
☐ shuffleboard ☐ pickleball ☐ golf

Camped with: _____

_____

_____

Places visited: _____

_____

_____

Visit/do next time: _____

_____

_____

Most memorable event:

Most fun things:

Notes:

Drawing or favorite photo:

Campground: _____ Dates: _____

Location: _____

Travel to Campground: *Miles:* _____ *Time:* _____ *Cost:* _____

Weather :

☀️ ⛅ ☁️ 🌧️ ⛈️ ❄️

☐ ☐ ☐ ☐ ☐ ☐

Campground Information

Name: _____

Address: _____

Phone: _____

Site#: _____ Site for next time: _____

Cost: _____ $ ☐ Day ☐ Week ☐ Month

GPS: _____

Rating: ★☆☆☆☆☆☆☆☆☆

Water pressure ★☆☆☆☆ Location ★☆☆☆☆

Cleanliness ★☆☆☆☆ Site size ★☆☆☆☆

Restrooms ★☆☆☆☆ Noise ★☆☆☆☆

Amenities:

☐ easy access ☐ back-in ☐ pull-through
☐ water ☐ pet friendly ☐ laundry
☐ paved ☐ sewer ☐ electricity
☐ 15 amp ☐ 30 amp ☐ 50 amp
☐ shade ☐ pool ☐ restrooms
☐ store ☐ picnic table ☐ fire ring
☐ firewood ☐ tv ☐ wifi
☐ security ☐ ice ☐ cafe

Activities:

☐ fishing ☐ hiking ☐ canoeing
☐ lake ☐ river ☐ hot tub
☐ fitness ☐ bike ☐ boat
☐ shuffleboard ☐ pickleball ☐ golf

Camped with: _____

_____

_____

Places visited: _____

_____

_____

Visit/do next time: _____

_____

_____

Most memorable event:

Most fun things:

Notes:

Drawing or favorite photo:

Campground: Dates:

Location:_____

Travel to Campground: *Miles:* _____ *Time:* _____ *Cost:* _____

Weather : ☀️ ⛅ ☁️ 🌧️ ⛈️ ❄️
☐ ☐ ☐ ☐ ☐ ☐

Campground Information

Name:_____

Address:_____

Phone:_____

Site#:_____ Site for next time:_____

Cost:_____ $ ☐ Day ☐ Week ☐ Month

GPS:_____

Rating: ★☆☆☆☆☆☆☆☆☆

Water pressure ★☆☆☆☆ Location ★☆☆☆☆

Cleanliness ★☆☆☆☆ Site size ★☆☆☆☆

Restrooms ★☆☆☆☆ Noise ★☆☆☆☆

Amenities:

☐ easy access	☐ back-in	☐ pull-through
☐ water	☐ pet friendly	☐ laundry
☐ paved	☐ sewer	☐ electricity
☐ 15 amp	☐ 30 amp	☐ 50 amp
☐ shade	☐ pool	☐ restrooms
☐ store	☐ picnic table	☐ fire ring
☐ firewood	☐ tv	☐ wifi
☐ security	☐ ice	☐ cafe

Activities:

☐ fishing	☐ hiking	☐ canoeing
☐ lake	☐ river	☐ hot tub
☐ fitness	☐ bike	☐ boat
☐ shuffleboard	☐ pickleball	☐ golf

Camped with:_____

_____

_____

Places visited:_____

_____

_____

Visit/do next time:_____

_____

_____

Most memorable event:

Most fun things:

Notes:

Drawing or favorite photo:

Campground: Dates:

Location:_____

Travel to Campground: *Miles:*_____ *Time:*_____ *Cost:*_____

Weather : ☀️ ⛅ ☁️ 🌧️ ⛈️ ❄️
☐ ☐ ☐ ☐ ☐ ☐

Campground Information

Name:_____

Address:_____

Phone:_____

Site#:_____ Site for next time:_____

Cost:_____ $ ☐ Day ☐Week ☐Month

GPS:_____

Rating: ★☆☆☆☆☆☆☆☆☆

Water pressure ★☆☆☆☆☆ **Location** ★☆☆☆☆☆

Cleanliness ★☆☆☆☆☆ **Site size** ★☆☆☆☆☆

Restrooms ★☆☆☆☆☆ **Noise** ★☆☆☆☆☆

Amenities:

☐ easy access   ☐ back-in   ☐ pull-through
☐ water   ☐ pet friendly   ☐ laundry
☐ paved   ☐ sewer   ☐ electricity
☐ 15 amp   ☐ 30 amp   ☐ 50 amp
☐ shade   ☐ pool   ☐ restrooms
☐ store   ☐ picnic table   ☐ fire ring
☐ firewood   ☐ tv   ☐ wifi
☐ security   ☐ ice   ☐ cafe

Activities:

☐ fishing   ☐ hiking   ☐ canoeing
☐ lake   ☐ river   ☐ hot tub
☐ fitness   ☐ bike   ☐ boat
☐ shuffleboard ☐ pickleball   ☐ golf

Camped with:_____

_____

_____

Places visited:_____

_____

_____

Visit/do next time:_____

_____

_____

Most memorable event:

Most fun things:

Notes:

Drawing or favorite photo:

Campground: **Dates:**

Location:_____

Travel to Campground: *Miles:* _____ *Time:* _____ *Cost:* _____

Weather : ☀️ ⛅ ☁️ 🌧️ ⛈️ ❄️
☐   ☐   ☐   ☐   ☐   ☐

Campground Information

Name:_____

Address:_____

Phone:_____

Site#:_____ Site for next time:_____

Cost:_____ $ ☐ Day ☐Week ☐Month

GPS:_____

Rating: ★☆☆☆☆☆☆☆☆☆

Water pressure ★☆☆☆☆ Location ★☆☆☆☆

Cleanliness ★☆☆☆☆ Site size ★☆☆☆☆

Restrooms ★☆☆☆☆ Noise ★☆☆☆☆

Amenities:

☐ easy access   ☐ back-in   ☐ pull-through
☐ water   ☐ pet friendly   ☐ laundry
☐ paved   ☐ sewer   ☐ electricity
☐ 15 amp   ☐ 30 amp   ☐ 50 amp
☐ shade   ☐ pool   ☐ restrooms
☐ store   ☐ picnic table   ☐ fire ring
☐ firewood   ☐ tv   ☐ wifi
☐ security   ☐ ice   ☐ cafe

Activities:

☐ fishing   ☐ hiking   ☐ canoeing
☐ lake   ☐ river   ☐ hot tub
☐ fitness   ☐ bike   ☐ boat
☐ shuffleboard   ☐ pickleball   ☐ golf

Camped with:_____

_____

Places visited:_____

_____

Visit/do next time:_____

_____

Most memorable event:

Most fun things:

Notes:

Drawing or favorite photo:

Campground: Dates:

Location:_____

Travel to Campground: *Miles:*_____ *Time:*_____ *Cost:*_____

Weather : ☀️ ⛅ ☁️ 🌧️ ⛈️ ❄️

☐   ☐   ☐   ☐   ☐   ☐

Campground Information

Name:_____

Address:_____

Phone:_____

Site#:_____ Site for next time:_____

Cost:_____ $ ☐ Day ☐Week ☐Month

GPS:_____

Rating: ★☆☆☆☆☆☆☆☆☆

Water pressure ★☆☆☆☆ Location ★☆☆☆☆

Cleanliness ★☆☆☆☆ Site size ★☆☆☆☆

Restrooms ★☆☆☆☆ Noise ★☆☆☆☆

Amenities:

☐ easy access   ☐ back-in   ☐ pull-through
☐ water   ☐ pet friendly   ☐ laundry
☐ paved   ☐ sewer   ☐ electricity
☐ 15 amp   ☐ 30 amp   ☐ 50 amp
☐ shade   ☐ pool   ☐ restrooms
☐ store   ☐ picnic table   ☐ fire ring
☐ firewood   ☐ tv   ☐ wifi
☐ security   ☐ ice   ☐ cafe

Activities:

☐ fishing   ☐ hiking   ☐ canoeing
☐ lake   ☐ river   ☐ hot tub
☐ fitness   ☐ bike   ☐ boat
☐ shuffleboard   ☐ pickleball   ☐ golf

Camped with:_____

_____

_____

Places visited:_____

_____

_____

Visit/do next time:_____

_____

_____

Most memorable event:

_____

_____

Most fun things:

_____

_____

_____

_____

Notes:

_____

_____

_____

_____

_____

Drawing or favorite photo:

Campground: _____ Dates: _____

Location: _____

Travel to Campground: *Miles:* _____ *Time:* _____ *Cost:* _____

Weather : ☀️ ⛅ ☁️ 🌧️ ⛈️ ❄️
⬜ ⬜ ⬜ ⬜ ⬜ ⬜

Campground Information

Name: _____

Address: _____

Phone: _____

Site#: _____ Site for next time: _____

Cost: _____ $ ⬜ Day ⬜Week ⬜Month

GPS: _____

Rating: ★☆☆☆☆☆☆☆☆☆

Water pressure ★☆☆☆☆☆ Location ★☆☆☆☆☆

Cleanliness ★☆☆☆☆☆ Site size ★☆☆☆☆☆

Restrooms ★☆☆☆☆☆ Noise ★☆☆☆☆☆

Amenities:

⬜ easy access	⬜ back-in	⬜ pull-through
⬜ water	⬜ pet friendly	⬜ laundry
⬜ paved	⬜ sewer	⬜ electricity
⬜ 15 amp	⬜ 30 amp	⬜ 50 amp
⬜ shade	⬜ pool	⬜ restrooms
⬜ store	⬜ picnic table	⬜ fire ring
⬜ firewood	⬜ tv	⬜ wifi
⬜ security	⬜ ice	⬜ cafe

Activities:

⬜ fishing	⬜ hiking	⬜ canoeing
⬜ lake	⬜ river	⬜ hot tub
⬜ fitness	⬜ bike	⬜ boat
⬜ shuffleboard	⬜ pickleball	⬜ golf

Camped with: _____

_____

_____

Places visited: _____

_____

_____

Visit/do next time: _____

_____

_____

Most memorable event:

Most fun things:

Notes:

Drawing or favorite photo:

Campground: _____   **Dates:** _____

Location: _____

Travel to Campground: *Miles:* _____ *Time:* _____ *Cost:* _____

Weather : ☀️ ⛅ ☁️ 🌧️ ⛈️ ❄️
☐ ☐ ☐ ☐ ☐ ☐

Campground Information

Name: _____

Address: _____

Phone: _____

Site#: _____ Site for next time: _____

Cost: _____ $ ☐ Day ☐ Week ☐ Month

GPS: _____

Rating: ★☆☆☆☆☆☆☆☆☆

Water pressure ★☆☆☆☆☆ Location ★☆☆☆☆☆

Cleanliness ★☆☆☆☆☆ Site size ★☆☆☆☆☆

Restrooms ★☆☆☆☆☆ Noise ★☆☆☆☆☆

Amenities:

☐ easy access   ☐ back-in   ☐ pull-through
☐ water   ☐ pet friendly   ☐ laundry
☐ paved   ☐ sewer   ☐ electricity
☐ 15 amp   ☐ 30 amp   ☐ 50 amp
☐ shade   ☐ pool   ☐ restrooms
☐ store   ☐ picnic table   ☐ fire ring
☐ firewood   ☐ tv   ☐ wifi
☐ security   ☐ ice   ☐ cafe

Activities:

☐ fishing   ☐ hiking   ☐ canoeing
☐ lake   ☐ river   ☐ hot tub
☐ fitness   ☐ bike   ☐ boat
☐ shuffleboard ☐ pickleball   ☐ golf

Camped with: _____

_____

Places visited: _____

_____

Visit/do next time: _____

_____

Most memorable event:

Most fun things:

Notes:

Drawing or favorite photo:

Campground: _____ **Dates:** _____

Location: _____

Travel to Campground: *Miles:* _____ *Time:* _____ *Cost:* _____

Weather : ☀️ ⛅ ☁️ 🌧️ ⛈️ ❄️
⬜ ⬜ ⬜ ⬜ ⬜ ⬜

Campground Information

Name: _____

Address: _____

Phone: _____

Site#: _____ Site for next time: _____

Cost: _____ $ ☐ Day ☐ Week ☐ Month

GPS: _____

Rating: ★☆☆☆☆☆☆☆☆☆

Water pressure ★☆☆☆☆☆ Location ★☆☆☆☆☆

Cleanliness ★☆☆☆☆☆ Site size ★☆☆☆☆☆

Restrooms ★☆☆☆☆☆ Noise ★☆☆☆☆☆

Amenities:

☐ easy access	☐ back-in	☐ pull-through
☐ water	☐ pet friendly	☐ laundry
☐ paved	☐ sewer	☐ electricity
☐ 15 amp	☐ 30 amp	☐ 50 amp
☐ shade	☐ pool	☐ restrooms
☐ store	☐ picnic table	☐ fire ring
☐ firewood	☐ tv	☐ wifi
☐ security	☐ ice	☐ cafe

Activities:

☐ fishing	☐ hiking	☐ canoeing
☐ lake	☐ river	☐ hot tub
☐ fitness	☐ bike	☐ boat
☐ shuffleboard	☐ pickleball	☐ golf

Camped with: _____

_____

_____

Places visited: _____

_____

_____

Visit/do next time: _____

_____

_____

Most memorable event:

Most fun things:

Notes:

Drawing or favorite photo:

Campground: _____ **Dates:** _____

Location:_____

Travel to Campground: *Miles:* _____ *Time:* _____ *Cost:* _____

Weather : ☀️ ⛅ ☁️ 🌧️ ⛈️ ❄️

◻ ◻ ◻ ◻ ◻ ◻

Campground Information

Name:_____

Address:_____

Phone:_____

Site#:_____ Site for next time:_____

Cost:_____ $ ◻ Day ◻Week ◻Month

GPS:_____

Rating: ★☆☆☆☆☆☆☆☆☆

Water pressure ★☆☆☆☆☆ Location ★☆☆☆☆☆

Cleanliness ★☆☆☆☆☆ Site size ★☆☆☆☆☆

Restrooms ★☆☆☆☆☆ Noise ★☆☆☆☆☆

Amenities:

◻ easy access ◻ back-in ◻ pull-through
◻ water ◻ pet friendly ◻ laundry
◻ paved ◻ sewer ◻ electricity
◻ 15 amp ◻ 30 amp ◻ 50 amp
◻ shade ◻ pool ◻ restrooms
◻ store ◻ picnic table ◻ fire ring
◻ firewood ◻ tv ◻ wifi
◻ security ◻ ice ◻ cafe

Activities:

◻ fishing ◻ hiking ◻ canoeing
◻ lake ◻ river ◻ hot tub
◻ fitness ◻ bike ◻ boat
◻ shuffleboard ◻ pickleball ◻ golf

Camped with:_____

_____

_____

Places visited:_____

_____

_____

Visit/do next time:_____

_____

_____

Most memorable event:

Most fun things:

Notes:

Drawing or favorite photo:

Campground: Dates:

Location: _____

Travel to Campground: *Miles:* _____ *Time:* _____ *Cost:* _____

Weather : ☀️ ☐   ⛅ ☐   ☁️ ☐   🌧️ ☐   ⛈️ ☐   ❄️ ☐

Campground Information

Name: _____

Address: _____

Phone: _____

Site#: _____ Site for next time: _____

Cost: _____ $ ☐ Day ☐ Week ☐ Month

GPS: _____

Rating: ★☆☆☆☆☆☆☆☆☆

Water pressure ★☆☆☆☆ Location ★☆☆☆☆

Cleanliness ★☆☆☆☆ Site size ★☆☆☆☆

Restrooms ★☆☆☆☆ Noise ★☆☆☆☆

Amenities:

☐ easy access   ☐ back-in   ☐ pull-through
☐ water   ☐ pet friendly   ☐ laundry
☐ paved   ☐ sewer   ☐ electricity
☐ 15 amp   ☐ 30 amp   ☐ 50 amp
☐ shade   ☐ pool   ☐ restrooms
☐ store   ☐ picnic table   ☐ fire ring
☐ firewood   ☐ tv   ☐ wifi
☐ security   ☐ ice   ☐ cafe

Activities:

☐ fishing   ☐ hiking   ☐ canoeing
☐ lake   ☐ river   ☐ hot tub
☐ fitness   ☐ bike   ☐ boat
☐ shuffleboard   ☐ pickleball   ☐ golf

Camped with: _____

_____

Places visited: _____

_____

_____

Visit/do next time: _____

_____

_____

Most memorable event:

_____

_____

Most fun things:

_____

_____

_____

Notes:

_____

_____

_____

_____

_____

Drawing or favorite photo:

Campground: _____ **Dates:** _____

Location:_____

Travel to Campground: *Miles:* _____ *Time:* _____ *Cost:* _____

Weather : ☀️ ⛅ ☁️ 🌧️ ⛈️ ❄️
☐ ☐ ☐ ☐ ☐ ☐

Campground Information

Name:_____

Address:_____

Phone:_____

Site#:_____ Site for next time:_____

Cost:_____ $ ☐ Day ☐Week ☐Month

GPS:_____

Rating: ★☆☆☆☆☆☆☆☆☆

Water pressure ★☆☆☆☆ Location ★☆☆☆☆

Cleanliness ★☆☆☆☆ Site size ★☆☆☆☆

Restrooms ★☆☆☆☆ Noise ★☆☆☆☆

Amenities:

☐ easy access ☐ back-in ☐ pull-through
☐ water ☐ pet friendly ☐ laundry
☐ paved ☐ sewer ☐ electricity
☐ 15 amp ☐ 30 amp ☐ 50 amp
☐ shade ☐ pool ☐ restrooms
☐ store ☐ picnic table ☐ fire ring
☐ firewood ☐ tv ☐ wifi
☐ security ☐ ice ☐ cafe

Activities:

☐ fishing ☐ hiking ☐ canoeing
☐ lake ☐ river ☐ hot tub
☐ fitness ☐ bike ☐ boat
☐ shuffleboard ☐ pickleball ☐ golf

Camped with:_____

_____

_____

Places visited:_____

_____

_____

Visit/do next time:_____

_____

_____

Most memorable event:

Most fun things:

Notes:

Drawing or favorite photo:

Campground: _____ **Dates:** _____

Location: _____

Travel to Campground: *Miles:* _____ *Time:* _____ *Cost:* _____

Weather : ☀️ ⛅ ☁️ 🌧️ ⛈️ ❄️
☐ ☐ ☐ ☐ ☐ ☐

Campground Information

Name: _____

Address: _____

Phone: _____

Site#: _____ **Site for next time:** _____

Cost: _____ $ ☐ Day ☐Week ☐Month

GPS: _____

Rating: ⭐☆☆☆☆☆☆☆☆☆

Water pressure ⭐☆☆☆☆☆ **Location** ⭐☆☆☆☆☆

Cleanliness ⭐☆☆☆☆☆ **Site size** ⭐☆☆☆☆☆

Restrooms ⭐☆☆☆☆☆ **Noise** ⭐☆☆☆☆☆

Amenities:

☐ easy access ☐ back-in ☐ pull-through
☐ water ☐ pet friendly ☐ laundry
☐ paved ☐ sewer ☐ electricity
☐ 15 amp ☐ 30 amp ☐ 50 amp
☐ shade ☐ pool ☐ restrooms
☐ store ☐ picnic table ☐ fire ring
☐ firewood ☐ tv ☐ wifi
☐ security ☐ ice ☐ cafe

Activities:

☐ fishing ☐ hiking ☐ canoeing
☐ lake ☐ river ☐ hot tub
☐ fitness ☐ bike ☐ boat
☐ shuffleboard ☐ pickleball ☐ golf

Camped with: _____

_____

Places visited: _____

_____

Visit/do next time: _____

_____

Most memorable event:

Most fun things:

Notes:

Drawing or favorite photo:

Campground: _____ Dates: _____

Location: _____

Travel to Campground: *Miles:* _____ *Time:* _____ *Cost:* _____

Weather : ☀️ ⛅ ☁️ 🌧️ ⛈️ ❄️
□　　□　　□　　□　　□　　□

Campground Information

Name: _____

Address: _____

Phone: _____

Site#: _____ Site for next time: _____

Cost: _____ $ □ Day □Week □Month

GPS: _____

Rating: ★☆☆☆☆☆☆☆☆☆

Water pressure ★☆☆☆☆ Location ★☆☆☆☆

Cleanliness ★☆☆☆☆ Site size ★☆☆☆☆

Restrooms ★☆☆☆☆ Noise ★☆☆☆☆

Amenities:

□ easy access　□ back-in　□ pull-through
□ water　　　　□ pet friendly　□ laundry
□ paved　　　　□ sewer　　　□ electricity
□ 15 amp　　　□ 30 amp　　□ 50 amp
□ shade　　　　□ pool　　　□ restrooms
□ store　　　　□ picnic table　□ fire ring
□ firewood　　□ tv　　　　□ wifi
□ security　　　□ ice　　　□ cafe

Activities:

□ fishing　　　□ hiking　　□ canoeing
□ lake　　　　□ river　　　□ hot tub
□ fitness　　　□ bike　　　□ boat
□ shuffleboard　□ pickleball　□ golf

Camped with: _____

_____

_____

Places visited: _____

_____

_____

Visit/do next time: _____

_____

_____

Most memorable event:

Most fun things:

Notes:

Drawing or favorite photo:

Campground: _____ **Dates:** _____

Location: _____

Travel to Campground: *Miles:* _____ *Time:* _____ *Cost:* _____

Weather : ☀️ ⛅ ☁️ 🌧️ ⛈️ ❄️
☐ ☐ ☐ ☐ ☐ ☐

Campground Information

Name: _____

Address: _____

Phone: _____

Site#: _____ Site for next time: _____

Cost: _____ $ ☐ Day ☐ Week ☐ Month

GPS: _____

Rating: ★☆☆☆☆☆☆☆☆☆

Water pressure ★☆☆☆☆ **Location** ★☆☆☆☆

Cleanliness ★☆☆☆☆ **Site size** ★☆☆☆☆

Restrooms ★☆☆☆☆ **Noise** ★☆☆☆☆

Amenities:

☐ easy access ☐ back-in ☐ pull-through
☐ water ☐ pet friendly ☐ laundry
☐ paved ☐ sewer ☐ electricity
☐ 15 amp ☐ 30 amp ☐ 50 amp
☐ shade ☐ pool ☐ restrooms
☐ store ☐ picnic table ☐ fire ring
☐ firewood ☐ tv ☐ wifi
☐ security ☐ ice ☐ cafe

Activities:

☐ fishing ☐ hiking ☐ canoeing
☐ lake ☐ river ☐ hot tub
☐ fitness ☐ bike ☐ boat
☐ shuffleboard ☐ pickleball ☐ golf

Camped with: _____

_____

Places visited: _____

_____

Visit/do next time: _____

_____

Most memorable event:

_____

_____

Most fun things:

_____

_____

_____

Notes:

_____

_____

_____

_____

Drawing or favorite photo:

Campground:	Dates:

Location:_____

Travel to Campground: *Miles:* _____ *Time:* _____ *Cost:* _____

Weather : ☀️ ⛅ ☁️ 🌧️ ⛈️ ❄️

⬜ ⬜ ⬜ ⬜ ⬜ ⬜

Campground Information

Name:_____

Address:_____

Phone:_____

Site#:_____ Site for next time:_____

Cost:_____ $ ⬜ Day ⬜Week ⬜Month

GPS:_____

Rating: ★☆☆☆☆☆☆☆☆☆

Water pressure ★☆☆☆☆ Location ★☆☆☆☆

Cleanliness ★☆☆☆☆ Site size ★☆☆☆☆

Restrooms ★☆☆☆☆ Noise ★☆☆☆☆

Amenities:

⬜ easy access	⬜ back-in	⬜ pull-through
⬜ water	⬜ pet friendly	⬜ laundry
⬜ paved	⬜ sewer	⬜ electricity
⬜ 15 amp	⬜ 30 amp	⬜ 50 amp
⬜ shade	⬜ pool	⬜ restrooms
⬜ store	⬜ picnic table	⬜ fire ring
⬜ firewood	⬜ tv	⬜ wifi
⬜ security	⬜ ice	⬜ cafe

Activities:

⬜ fishing	⬜ hiking	⬜ canoeing
⬜ lake	⬜ river	⬜ hot tub
⬜ fitness	⬜ bike	⬜ boat
⬜ shuffleboard	⬜ pickleball	⬜ golf

Camped with:_____

_____

_____

Places visited:_____

_____

_____

Visit/do next time:_____

_____

_____

Most memorable event:

Most fun things:

Notes:

Drawing or favorite photo:

Campground: _____ Dates: _____

Location: _____

Travel to Campground: *Miles:* _____ *Time:* _____ *Cost:* _____

Weather : ☀️ ☐ ⛅ ☐ ☁️ ☐ 🌧️ ☐ ⛈️ ☐ ❄️ ☐

Campground Information

Name: _____

Address: _____

Phone: _____

Site#: _____ Site for next time: _____

Cost: _____ $ ☐ Day ☐ Week ☐ Month

GPS: _____

Rating: ★☆☆☆☆☆☆☆☆☆

Water pressure ★☆☆☆☆ Location ★☆☆☆☆

Cleanliness ★☆☆☆☆ Site size ★☆☆☆☆

Restrooms ★☆☆☆☆ Noise ★☆☆☆☆

Amenities:

☐ easy access ☐ back-in ☐ pull-through
☐ water ☐ pet friendly ☐ laundry
☐ paved ☐ sewer ☐ electricity
☐ 15 amp ☐ 30 amp ☐ 50 amp
☐ shade ☐ pool ☐ restrooms
☐ store ☐ picnic table ☐ fire ring
☐ firewood ☐ tv ☐ wifi
☐ security ☐ ice ☐ cafe

Activities:

☐ fishing ☐ hiking ☐ canoeing
☐ lake ☐ river ☐ hot tub
☐ fitness ☐ bike ☐ boat
☐ shuffleboard ☐ pickleball ☐ golf

Camped with: _____
_____
_____

Places visited: _____
_____
_____

Visit/do next time: _____
_____
_____

Most memorable event:

Most fun things:

Notes:

Drawing or favorite photo:

Campground: _____ **Dates:** _____

Location: _____

Travel to Campground: *Miles:* _____ *Time:* _____ *Cost:* _____

Weather : ☐ ☐ ☐ ☐ ☐ ☐

Campground Information

Name: _____

Address: _____

Phone: _____

Site#: _____ **Site for next time:** _____

Cost: _____ $ ☐ Day ☐Week ☐Month

GPS: _____

Rating: ★☆☆☆☆☆☆☆☆☆

Water pressure ★☆☆☆☆ **Location** ★☆☆☆☆

Cleanliness ★☆☆☆☆ **Site size** ★☆☆☆☆

Restrooms ★☆☆☆☆ **Noise** ★☆☆☆☆

Amenities:

☐ easy access ☐ back-in ☐ pull-through
☐ water ☐ pet friendly ☐ laundry
☐ paved ☐ sewer ☐ electricity
☐ 15 amp ☐ 30 amp ☐ 50 amp
☐ shade ☐ pool ☐ restrooms
☐ store ☐ picnic table ☐ fire ring
☐ firewood ☐ tv ☐ wifi
☐ security ☐ ice ☐ cafe

Activities:

☐ fishing ☐ hiking ☐ canoeing
☐ lake ☐ river ☐ hot tub
☐ fitness ☐ bike ☐ boat
☐ shuffleboard ☐ pickleball ☐ golf

Camped with: _____

_____

Places visited: _____

_____

Visit/do next time: _____

_____

Most memorable event:

Most fun things:

Notes:

Drawing or favorite photo:

Campground:

Dates:

Location:_____

Travel to Campground: *Miles:*_____ *Time:*_____ *Cost:*_____

Weather :

☐ ☐ ☐ ☐ ☐ ☐

Campground Information

Name:_____

Address:_____

Phone:_____

Site#:_____ Site for next time:_____

Cost:_____ $ ☐ Day ☐Week ☐Month

GPS:_____

Rating: ★☆☆☆☆☆☆☆☆☆

Water pressure ★☆☆☆☆☆ **Location** ★☆☆☆☆☆

Cleanliness ★☆☆☆☆☆ **Site size** ★☆☆☆☆☆

Restrooms ★☆☆☆☆☆ **Noise** ★☆☆☆☆☆

Amenities:

☐ easy access ☐ back-in ☐ pull-through
☐ water ☐ pet friendly ☐ laundry
☐ paved ☐ sewer ☐ electricity
☐ 15 amp ☐ 30 amp ☐ 50 amp
☐ shade ☐ pool ☐ restrooms
☐ store ☐ picnic table ☐ fire ring
☐ firewood ☐ tv ☐ wifi
☐ security ☐ ice ☐ cafe

Activities:

☐ fishing ☐ hiking ☐ canoeing
☐ lake ☐ river ☐ hot tub
☐ fitness ☐ bike ☐ boat
☐ shuffleboard ☐ pickleball ☐ golf

Camped with:_____

_____

Places visited:_____

_____

Visit/do next time:_____

_____

Most memorable event:

Most fun things:

Notes:

Drawing or favorite photo:

Campground: Dates:

Location:_____

Travel to Campground: *Miles:*_____ *Time:*_____ *Cost:*_____

Weather : ☀️ ⛅ ☁️ 🌧️ ⛈️ ❄️
☐ ☐ ☐ ☐ ☐ ☐

Campground Information

Name:_____

Address:_____

Phone:_____

Site#:_____ Site for next time:_____

Cost:_____ $ ☐ Day ☐Week ☐Month

GPS:_____

Rating: ★☆☆☆☆☆☆☆☆☆

Water pressure ★☆☆☆☆ Location ★☆☆☆☆

Cleanliness ★☆☆☆☆ Site size ★☆☆☆☆

Restrooms ★☆☆☆☆ Noise ★☆☆☆☆

Amenities:

☐ easy access   ☐ back-in   ☐ pull-through
☐ water   ☐ pet friendly   ☐ laundry
☐ paved   ☐ sewer   ☐ electricity
☐ 15 amp   ☐ 30 amp   ☐ 50 amp
☐ shade   ☐ pool   ☐ restrooms
☐ store   ☐ picnic table   ☐ fire ring
☐ firewood   ☐ tv   ☐ wifi
☐ security   ☐ ice   ☐ cafe

Activities:

☐ fishing   ☐ hiking   ☐ canoeing
☐ lake   ☐ river   ☐ hot tub
☐ fitness   ☐ bike   ☐ boat
☐ shuffleboard   ☐ pickleball   ☐ golf

Camped with:_____

_____

_____

Places visited:_____

_____

_____

Visit/do next time:_____

_____

_____

Most memorable event:

Most fun things:

Notes:

Drawing or favorite photo:

Campground: Dates:

Location:_____

Travel to Campground: *Miles:*_____ *Time:*_____ *Cost:*_____

Weather : ☀ 🌤 ☁ 🌧 ⛈ ❄
⬜ ⬜ ⬜ ⬜ ⬜ ⬜

Campground Information

Name:_____

Address:_____

Phone:_____

Site#:_____ Site for next time:_____

Cost:_____ $ ☐ Day ☐Week ☐Month

GPS:_____

Rating: ★☆☆☆☆☆☆☆☆☆

Water pressure ★☆☆☆☆☆ Location ★☆☆☆☆

Cleanliness ★☆☆☆☆☆ Site size ★☆☆☆☆

Restrooms ★☆☆☆☆☆ Noise ★☆☆☆☆

Amenities:

☐ easy access ☐ back-in ☐ pull-through
☐ water ☐ pet friendly ☐ laundry
☐ paved ☐ sewer ☐ electricity
☐ 15 amp ☐ 30 amp ☐ 50 amp
☐ shade ☐ pool ☐ restrooms
☐ store ☐ picnic table ☐ fire ring
☐ firewood ☐ tv ☐ wifi
☐ security ☐ ice ☐ cafe

Activities:

☐ fishing ☐ hiking ☐ canoeing
☐ lake ☐ river ☐ hot tub
☐ fitness ☐ bike ☐ boat
☐ shuffleboard ☐ pickleball ☐ golf

Camped with:_____

_____

_____

Places visited:_____

_____

_____

Visit/do next time:_____

_____

_____

Most memorable event:

_____

Most fun things:

_____

_____

_____

Notes:

_____

_____

_____

_____

Drawing or favorite photo:

Campground: _____ Dates: _____

Location:_____

Travel to Campground: *Miles:* _____ *Time:* _____ *Cost:* _____

Weather : ☐ ☐ ☐ ☐ ☐ ☐

Campground Information

Name:_____

Address:_____

Phone:_____

Site#:_____ Site for next time: _____

Cost:_____ $ ☐ Day ☐Week ☐Month

GPS:_____

Rating: ★☆☆☆☆☆☆☆☆☆

Water pressure ★☆☆☆☆ Location ★☆☆☆☆

Cleanliness ★☆☆☆☆ Site size ★☆☆☆☆

Restrooms ★☆☆☆☆ Noise ★☆☆☆☆

Amenities:

☐ easy access ☐ back-in ☐ pull-through
☐ water ☐ pet friendly ☐ laundry
☐ paved ☐ sewer ☐ electricity
☐ 15 amp ☐ 30 amp ☐ 50 amp
☐ shade ☐ pool ☐ restrooms
☐ store ☐ picnic table ☐ fire ring
☐ firewood ☐ tv ☐ wifi
☐ security ☐ ice ☐ cafe

Activities:

☐ fishing ☐ hiking ☐ canoeing
☐ lake ☐ river ☐ hot tub
☐ fitness ☐ bike ☐ boat
☐ shuffleboard ☐ pickleball ☐ golf

Camped with:_____

_____

Places visited:_____

_____

Visit/do next time:_____

_____

Most memorable event:

_____

_____

Most fun things:

_____

_____

_____

Notes:

_____

_____

_____

_____

_____

Drawing or favorite photo:

Campground:

Dates:

Location:_____

Travel to Campground: *Miles:*_____ *Time:*_____ *Cost:*_____

Weather : ☐ ☐ ☐ ☐ ☐ ☐

Campground Information

Name:_____

Address:_____

Phone:_____

Site#:_____ Site for next time:_____

Cost:_____ $ ☐ Day ☐ Week ☐ Month

GPS:_____

Rating: ★☆☆☆☆☆☆☆☆☆

Water pressure ★☆☆☆☆ Location ★☆☆☆☆

Cleanliness ★☆☆☆☆ Site size ★☆☆☆☆

Restrooms ★☆☆☆☆ Noise ★☆☆☆☆

Amenities:

☐ easy access	☐ back-in	☐ pull-through
☐ water	☐ pet friendly	☐ laundry
☐ paved	☐ sewer	☐ electricity
☐ 15 amp	☐ 30 amp	☐ 50 amp
☐ shade	☐ pool	☐ restrooms
☐ store	☐ picnic table	☐ fire ring
☐ firewood	☐ tv	☐ wifi
☐ security	☐ ice	☐ cafe

Activities:

☐ fishing	☐ hiking	☐ canoeing
☐ lake	☐ river	☐ hot tub
☐ fitness	☐ bike	☐ boat
☐ shuffleboard	☐ pickleball	☐ golf

Camped with:_____

_____

Places visited:_____

_____

Visit/do next time:_____

_____

Most memorable event:

_____

_____

Most fun things:

_____

_____

_____

Notes:

_____

_____

_____

_____

_____

Drawing or favorite photo:

Campground: _____ **Dates:** _____

Location: _____

Travel to Campground: *Miles:* _____ *Time:* _____ *Cost:* _____

Weather: ☀️ 🌤️ ☁️ 🌧️ ⛈️ ❄️
⬜ ⬜ ⬜ ⬜ ⬜ ⬜

Campground Information

Name: _____

Address: _____

Phone: _____

Site#: _____ Site for next time: _____

Cost: _____ $ ☐ Day ☐Week ☐Month

GPS: _____

Rating: ★☆☆☆☆☆☆☆☆☆

Water pressure ★☆☆☆☆ Location ★☆☆☆☆

Cleanliness ★☆☆☆☆ Site size ★☆☆☆☆

Restrooms ★☆☆☆☆ Noise ★☆☆☆☆

Amenities:

☐ easy access	☐ back-in	☐ pull-through
☐ water	☐ pet friendly	☐ laundry
☐ paved	☐ sewer	☐ electricity
☐ 15 amp	☐ 30 amp	☐ 50 amp
☐ shade	☐ pool	☐ restrooms
☐ store	☐ picnic table	☐ fire ring
☐ firewood	☐ tv	☐ wifi
☐ security	☐ ice	☐ cafe

Activities:

☐ fishing	☐ hiking	☐ canoeing
☐ lake	☐ river	☐ hot tub
☐ fitness	☐ bike	☐ boat
☐ shuffleboard	☐ pickleball	☐ golf

Camped with: _____

_____

Places visited: _____

_____

Visit/do next time: _____

_____

Most memorable event:

_____

_____

Most fun things:

_____

_____

_____

Notes:

_____

_____

_____

_____

Drawing or favorite photo:

Campground: _____   Dates: _____

Location: _____

Travel to Campground: *Miles:* _____ *Time:* _____ *Cost:* _____

Weather : ☐ ☐ ☐ ☐ ☐ ☐

Campground Information

Name: _____

Address: _____

Phone: _____

Site#: _____ Site for next time: _____

Cost: _____ $ ☐ Day ☐Week ☐Month

GPS: _____

Rating: ★☆☆☆☆☆☆☆☆☆

Water pressure ★☆☆☆☆☆ **Location** ★☆☆☆☆☆

Cleanliness ★☆☆☆☆☆ **Site size** ★☆☆☆☆☆

Restrooms ★☆☆☆☆☆ **Noise** ★☆☆☆☆☆

Amenities:

☐ easy access	☐ back-in	☐ pull-through
☐ water	☐ pet friendly	☐ laundry
☐ paved	☐ sewer	☐ electricity
☐ 15 amp	☐ 30 amp	☐ 50 amp
☐ shade	☐ pool	☐ restrooms
☐ store	☐ picnic table	☐ fire ring
☐ firewood	☐ tv	☐ wifi
☐ security	☐ ice	☐ cafe

Activities:

☐ fishing	☐ hiking	☐ canoeing
☐ lake	☐ river	☐ hot tub
☐ fitness	☐ bike	☐ boat
☐ shuffleboard	☐ pickleball	☐ golf

Camped with: _____

_____

Places visited: _____

_____

Visit/do next time: _____

_____

Most memorable event:

Most fun things:

Notes:

Drawing or favorite photo:

Campground: Dates:

Location:_____

Travel to Campground: *Miles:* _____ *Time:* _____ *Cost:* _____

Weather :   ☐   ☐   ☐   ☐   ☐   ☐

Campground Information

Name:_____	**Amenities:**
Address:_____	☐ easy access ☐ back-in ☐ pull-through
Phone:_____	☐ water ☐ pet friendly ☐ laundry
Site#:_____ Site for next time:_____	☐ paved ☐ sewer ☐ electricity
	☐ 15 amp ☐ 30 amp ☐ 50 amp
Cost:_____ $ ☐ Day ☐Week ☐Month	☐ shade ☐ pool ☐ restrooms
	☐ store ☐ picnic table ☐ fire ring
GPS:_____	☐ firewood ☐ tv ☐ wifi
	☐ security ☐ ice ☐ cafe

Rating: ★☆☆☆☆☆☆☆☆☆

Water pressure ★☆☆☆☆ Location ★☆☆☆☆

Cleanliness ★☆☆☆☆ Site size ★☆☆☆☆

Restrooms ★☆☆☆☆ Noise ★☆☆☆☆

Activities:

☐ fishing ☐ hiking ☐ canoeing
☐ lake ☐ river ☐ hot tub
☐ fitness ☐ bike ☐ boat
☐ shuffleboard ☐ pickleball ☐ golf

Camped with:_____

_____

Places visited:_____

_____

Visit/do next time:_____

_____

Most memorable event:

Most fun things:

Notes:

Drawing or favorite photo:

Campground: _____ Dates: _____

Location: _____

Travel to Campground: *Miles:* _____ *Time:* _____ *Cost:* _____

Weather: ☀️ ⛅ ☁️ 🌧️ ⛈️ ❄️
☐ ☐ ☐ ☐ ☐ ☐

Campground Information

Name: _____

Address: _____

Phone: _____

Site#: _____ Site for next time: _____

Cost: _____ $ ☐ Day ☐ Week ☐ Month

GPS: _____

Rating: ★☆☆☆☆☆☆☆☆☆

Water pressure ★☆☆☆☆☆ Location ★☆☆☆☆☆

Cleanliness ★☆☆☆☆☆ Site size ★☆☆☆☆☆

Restrooms ★☆☆☆☆☆ Noise ★☆☆☆☆☆

Amenities:

☐ easy access ☐ back-in ☐ pull-through
☐ water ☐ pet friendly ☐ laundry
☐ paved ☐ sewer ☐ electricity
☐ 15 amp ☐ 30 amp ☐ 50 amp
☐ shade ☐ pool ☐ restrooms
☐ store ☐ picnic table ☐ fire ring
☐ firewood ☐ tv ☐ wifi
☐ security ☐ ice ☐ cafe

Activities:

☐ fishing ☐ hiking ☐ canoeing
☐ lake ☐ river ☐ hot tub
☐ fitness ☐ bike ☐ boat
☐ shuffleboard ☐ pickleball ☐ golf

Camped with: _____
_____
_____

Places visited: _____
_____
_____

Visit/do next time: _____
_____
_____

Most memorable event:

_____

Most fun things:

_____

_____

_____

Notes:

_____

_____

_____

_____

_____

Drawing or favorite photo:

Campground: Dates:

Location:_____

Travel to Campground: *Miles:*_____ *Time:*_____ *Cost:*_____

Weather : ☐ ☐ ☐ ☐ ☐ ☐

Campground Information

Name:_____

Address:_____

Phone:_____

Site#:_____ Site for next time:_____

Cost:_____ $ ☐ Day ☐Week ☐Month

GPS:_____

Rating: ★☆☆☆☆☆☆☆☆☆

Water pressure ★☆☆☆☆ Location ★☆☆☆☆

Cleanliness ★☆☆☆☆ Site size ★☆☆☆☆

Restrooms ★☆☆☆☆ Noise ★☆☆☆☆

Amenities:

☐ easy access ☐ back-in ☐ pull-through
☐ water ☐ pet friendly ☐ laundry
☐ paved ☐ sewer ☐ electricity
☐ 15 amp ☐ 30 amp ☐ 50 amp
☐ shade ☐ pool ☐ restrooms
☐ store ☐ picnic table ☐ fire ring
☐ firewood ☐ tv ☐ wifi
☐ security ☐ ice ☐ cafe

Activities:

☐ fishing ☐ hiking ☐ canoeing
☐ lake ☐ river ☐ hot tub
☐ fitness ☐ bike ☐ boat
☐ shuffleboard ☐ pickleball ☐ golf

Camped with:_____

_____

_____

Places visited:_____

_____

_____

Visit/do next time:_____

_____

_____

Most memorable event:

_____

_____

Most fun things:

_____

_____

_____

Notes:

_____

_____

_____

_____

Drawing or favorite photo:

Campground: _____ **Dates:** _____

Location: _____

Travel to Campground: *Miles:* _____ *Time:* _____ *Cost:* _____

Weather : ☀️ ⛅ ☁️ 🌧️ ⛈️ ❄️
☐ ☐ ☐ ☐ ☐ ☐

Campground Information

Name: _____

Address: _____

Phone: _____

Site#: _____ Site for next time: _____

Cost: _____ $ ☐ Day ☐Week ☐Month

GPS: _____

Rating: ★☆☆☆☆☆☆☆☆☆

Water pressure ★☆☆☆☆ Location ★☆☆☆☆

Cleanliness ★☆☆☆☆ Site size ★☆☆☆☆

Restrooms ★☆☆☆☆ Noise ★☆☆☆☆

Amenities:

☐ easy access ☐ back-in ☐ pull-through
☐ water ☐ pet friendly ☐ laundry
☐ paved ☐ sewer ☐ electricity
☐ 15 amp ☐ 30 amp ☐ 50 amp
☐ shade ☐ pool ☐ restrooms
☐ store ☐ picnic table ☐ fire ring
☐ firewood ☐ tv ☐ wifi
☐ security ☐ ice ☐ cafe

Activities:

☐ fishing ☐ hiking ☐ canoeing
☐ lake ☐ river ☐ hot tub
☐ fitness ☐ bike ☐ boat
☐ shuffleboard ☐ pickleball ☐ golf

Camped with: _____

_____

_____

Places visited: _____

_____

_____

Visit/do next time: _____

_____

_____

Most memorable event:

Most fun things:

Notes:

Drawing or favorite photo:

Campground: Dates:

Location:_____

Travel to Campground: *Miles:* _____ *Time:* _____ *Cost:* _____

Weather : ☐ ☐ ☐ ☐ ☐ ☐

Campground Information

Name:_____

Address:_____

Phone:_____

Site#:_____ Site for next time:_____

Cost:_____ $ ☐ Day ☐Week ☐Month

GPS:_____

Rating: ★☆☆☆☆☆☆☆☆☆

Water pressure ★☆☆☆☆ Location ★☆☆☆☆

Cleanliness ★☆☆☆☆ Site size ★☆☆☆☆

Restrooms ★☆☆☆☆ Noise ★☆☆☆☆

Amenities:

☐ easy access ☐ back-in ☐ pull-through
☐ water ☐ pet friendly ☐ laundry
☐ paved ☐ sewer ☐ electricity
☐ 15 amp ☐ 30 amp ☐ 50 amp
☐ shade ☐ pool ☐ restrooms
☐ store ☐ picnic table ☐ fire ring
☐ firewood ☐ tv ☐ wifi
☐ security ☐ ice ☐ cafe

Activities:

☐ fishing ☐ hiking ☐ canoeing
☐ lake ☐ river ☐ hot tub
☐ fitness ☐ bike ☐ boat
☐ shuffleboard ☐ pickleball ☐ golf

Camped with:_____

_____

_____

Places visited:_____

_____

_____

Visit/do next time:_____

_____

_____

Most memorable event:_____

_____

Most fun things:_____

_____

_____

Notes:_____

_____

_____

_____

_____

Drawing or favorite photo:

Campground: Dates:

Location:_____

Travel to Campground: *Miles:* _____ *Time:* _____ *Cost:* _____

Weather : ☀️ ⛅ ☁️ 🌧️ ⛈️ ❄️
☐ ☐ ☐ ☐ ☐ ☐

Campground Information

Name:_____

Address:_____

Phone:_____

Site#:_____ Site for next time:_____

Cost:_____ $ ☐ Day ☐ Week ☐ Month

GPS:_____

Rating: ★☆☆☆☆☆☆☆☆☆

Water pressure ★☆☆☆☆ Location ★☆☆☆☆

Cleanliness ★☆☆☆☆ Site size ★☆☆☆☆

Restrooms ★☆☆☆☆ Noise ★☆☆☆☆

Amenities:

☐ easy access	☐ back-in	☐ pull-through
☐ water	☐ pet friendly	☐ laundry
☐ paved	☐ sewer	☐ electricity
☐ 15 amp	☐ 30 amp	☐ 50 amp
☐ shade	☐ pool	☐ restrooms
☐ store	☐ picnic table	☐ fire ring
☐ firewood	☐ tv	☐ wifi
☐ security	☐ ice	☐ cafe

Activities:

☐ fishing	☐ hiking	☐ canoeing
☐ lake	☐ river	☐ hot tub
☐ fitness	☐ bike	☐ boat
☐ shuffleboard	☐ pickleball	☐ golf

Camped with:_____

_____

Places visited:_____

_____

Visit/do next time:_____

_____

Most memorable event:_____

_____

Most fun things:_____

_____

_____

_____

Notes:_____

_____

_____

_____

_____

_____

Drawing or favorite photo:

Campground: **Dates:**

Location:_____

Travel to Campground: *Miles:* _____ *Time:* _____ *Cost:* _____

Weather : ☀️ ⛅ ☁️ 🌧️ ⛈️ ❄️
☐ ☐ ☐ ☐ ☐ ☐

Campground Information

Name:_____

Address:_____

Phone:_____

Site#:_____ Site for next time:_____

Cost:_____ $ ☐ Day ☐Week ☐Month

GPS:_____

Rating: ★☆☆☆☆☆☆☆☆☆

Water pressure ★☆☆☆☆ Location ★☆☆☆☆

Cleanliness ★☆☆☆☆ Site size ★☆☆☆☆

Restrooms ★☆☆☆☆ Noise ★☆☆☆☆

Amenities:

☐ easy access   ☐ back-in   ☐ pull-through
☐ water   ☐ pet friendly   ☐ laundry
☐ paved   ☐ sewer   ☐ electricity
☐ 15 amp   ☐ 30 amp   ☐ 50 amp
☐ shade   ☐ pool   ☐ restrooms
☐ store   ☐ picnic table   ☐ fire ring
☐ firewood   ☐ tv   ☐ wifi
☐ security   ☐ ice   ☐ cafe

Activities:

☐ fishing   ☐ hiking   ☐ canoeing
☐ lake   ☐ river   ☐ hot tub
☐ fitness   ☐ bike   ☐ boat
☐ shuffleboard   ☐ pickleball   ☐ golf

Camped with:_____

_____

_____

Places visited:_____

_____

_____

Visit/do next time:_____

_____

_____

Most memorable event:

Most fun things:

Notes:

Drawing or favorite photo:

Campground:	Dates:

Location:_____

Travel to Campground: *Miles:* _____ *Time:* _____ *Cost:* _____

Weather : ☀️ ⛅ ☁️ 🌧️ ⛈️ ❄️

☐ ☐ ☐ ☐ ☐ ☐

Campground Information

Name:_____

Address:_____

Phone:_____

Site#:_____ Site for next time:_____

Cost:_____ $ ☐ Day ☐Week ☐Month

GPS:_____

Rating: ★☆☆☆☆☆☆☆☆☆

Water pressure ★☆☆☆☆ Location ★☆☆☆☆

Cleanliness ★☆☆☆☆ Site size ★☆☆☆☆

Restrooms ★☆☆☆☆ Noise ★☆☆☆☆

Amenities:

☐ easy access ☐ back-in ☐ pull-through
☐ water ☐ pet friendly ☐ laundry
☐ paved ☐ sewer ☐ electricity
☐ 15 amp ☐ 30 amp ☐ 50 amp
☐ shade ☐ pool ☐ restrooms
☐ store ☐ picnic table ☐ fire ring
☐ firewood ☐ tv ☐ wifi
☐ security ☐ ice ☐ cafe

Activities:

☐ fishing ☐ hiking ☐ canoeing
☐ lake ☐ river ☐ hot tub
☐ fitness ☐ bike ☐ boat
☐ shuffleboard ☐ pickleball ☐ golf

Camped with:_____

_____

_____

Places visited:_____

_____

_____

Visit/do next time:_____

_____

_____

Most memorable event:

Most fun things:

Notes:

Drawing or favorite photo:

Campground: Dates:

Location:_____

Travel to Campground: *Miles:* _____ *Time:* _____ *Cost:* _____

Weather : ☀️ ⛅ ☁️ 🌧️ ⛈️ ❄️
☐   ☐   ☐   ☐   ☐   ☐

Campground Information

Name:_____

Address:_____

Phone:_____

Site#:_____ Site for next time:_____

Cost:_____ $ ☐ Day ☐Week ☐Month

GPS:_____

Rating: ★☆☆☆☆☆☆☆☆☆

Water pressure ★☆☆☆☆ Location ★☆☆☆☆

Cleanliness ★☆☆☆☆ Site size ★☆☆☆☆

Restrooms ★☆☆☆☆ Noise ★☆☆☆☆

Amenities:

☐ easy access   ☐ back-in   ☐ pull-through
☐ water   ☐ pet friendly   ☐ laundry
☐ paved   ☐ sewer   ☐ electricity
☐ 15 amp   ☐ 30 amp   ☐ 50 amp
☐ shade   ☐ pool   ☐ restrooms
☐ store   ☐ picnic table   ☐ fire ring
☐ firewood   ☐ tv   ☐ wifi
☐ security   ☐ ice   ☐ cafe

Activities:

☐ fishing   ☐ hiking   ☐ canoeing
☐ lake   ☐ river   ☐ hot tub
☐ fitness   ☐ bike   ☐ boat
☐ shuffleboard   ☐ pickleball   ☐ golf

Camped with:_____

_____

_____

Places visited:_____

_____

_____

Visit/do next time:_____

_____

_____

Most memorable event:

Most fun things:

Notes:

Drawing or favorite photo:

Campground: _____   Dates: _____

Location:_____

Travel to Campground: *Miles:* _____ *Time:* _____ *Cost:* _____

Weather : ☐ ☐ ☐ ☐ ☐ ☐

Campground Information

Name:_____

Address:_____

Phone:_____

Site#:_____ Site for next time:_____

Cost:_____ $ ☐ Day ☐ Week ☐ Month

GPS:_____

Rating: ★☆☆☆☆☆☆☆☆☆

Water pressure ★☆☆☆☆ Location ★☆☆☆☆

Cleanliness ★☆☆☆☆ Site size ★☆☆☆☆

Restrooms ★☆☆☆☆ Noise ★☆☆☆☆

Amenities:

☐ easy access	☐ back-in	☐ pull-through
☐ water	☐ pet friendly	☐ laundry
☐ paved	☐ sewer	☐ electricity
☐ 15 amp	☐ 30 amp	☐ 50 amp
☐ shade	☐ pool	☐ restrooms
☐ store	☐ picnic table	☐ fire ring
☐ firewood	☐ tv	☐ wifi
☐ security	☐ ice	☐ cafe

Activities:

☐ fishing	☐ hiking	☐ canoeing
☐ lake	☐ river	☐ hot tub
☐ fitness	☐ bike	☐ boat
☐ shuffleboard	☐ pickleball	☐ golf

Camped with:_____

_____

_____

Places visited:_____

_____

_____

Visit/do next time:_____

_____

_____

Most memorable event:

Most fun things:

Notes:

Drawing or favorite photo:

Campground: Dates:

Location:_____

Travel to Campground: *Miles:* _____ *Time:* _____ *Cost:* _____

Weather : ☐ ☐ ☐ ☐ ☐ ☐

Campground Information

Name:_____

Address:_____

Phone:_____

Site#:_____ Site for next time:_____

Cost:_____ $ ☐ Day ☐Week ☐Month

GPS:_____

Rating: ★☆☆☆☆☆☆☆☆☆

Water pressure ★☆☆☆☆☆ **Location** ★☆☆☆☆☆

Cleanliness ★☆☆☆☆☆ **Site size** ★☆☆☆☆☆

Restrooms ★☆☆☆☆☆ **Noise** ★☆☆☆☆☆

Amenities:

☐ easy access	☐ back-in	☐ pull-through
☐ water	☐ pet friendly	☐ laundry
☐ paved	☐ sewer	☐ electricity
☐ 15 amp	☐ 30 amp	☐ 50 amp
☐ shade	☐ pool	☐ restrooms
☐ store	☐ picnic table	☐ fire ring
☐ firewood	☐ tv	☐ wifi
☐ security	☐ ice	☐ cafe

Activities:

☐ fishing	☐ hiking	☐ canoeing
☐ lake	☐ river	☐ hot tub
☐ fitness	☐ bike	☐ boat
☐ shuffleboard	☐ pickleball	☐ golf

Camped with:_____

_____

Places visited:_____

_____

Visit/do next time:_____

_____

Most memorable event:

Most fun things:

Notes:

Drawing or favorite photo:

Campground: _____ Dates: _____

Location:_____

Travel to Campground: *Miles:* _____ *Time:* _____ *Cost:* _____

Weather :
☀ ☐ ⛅ ☐ ☁ ☐ 🌧 ☐ ⛈ ☐ ❄ ☐

Campground Information

Name:_____

Address:_____

Phone:_____

Site#:_____ Site for next time:_____

Cost:_____ $ ☐ Day ☐Week ☐Month

GPS:_____

Rating: ★☆☆☆☆☆☆☆☆☆

Water pressure ★☆☆☆☆ Location ★☆☆☆☆

Cleanliness ★☆☆☆☆ Site size ★☆☆☆☆

Restrooms ★☆☆☆☆ Noise ★☆☆☆☆

Amenities:

☐ easy access ☐ back-in ☐ pull-through
☐ water ☐ pet friendly ☐ laundry
☐ paved ☐ sewer ☐ electricity
☐ 15 amp ☐ 30 amp ☐ 50 amp
☐ shade ☐ pool ☐ restrooms
☐ store ☐ picnic table ☐ fire ring
☐ firewood ☐ tv ☐ wifi
☐ security ☐ ice ☐ cafe

Activities:

☐ fishing ☐ hiking ☐ canoeing
☐ lake ☐ river ☐ hot tub
☐ fitness ☐ bike ☐ boat
☐ shuffleboard ☐ pickleball ☐ golf

Camped with:_____
_____
_____

Places visited:_____
_____
_____

Visit/do next time:_____
_____
_____

Most memorable event:

Most fun things:

Notes:

Drawing or favorite photo:

Campground:

Dates:

Location:_____

Travel to Campground: *Miles:*_____ *Time:*_____ *Cost:*_____

Weather : ☐ ☐ ☐ ☐ ☐ ☐

Campground Information

Name:_____

Address:_____

Phone:_____

Site#:_____ Site for next time:_____

Cost:_____ $ ☐ Day ☐Week ☐Month

GPS:_____

Rating: ★☆☆☆☆☆☆☆☆☆

Water pressure ★☆☆☆☆ Location ★☆☆☆☆

Cleanliness ★☆☆☆☆ Site size ★☆☆☆☆

Restrooms ★☆☆☆☆ Noise ★☆☆☆☆

Amenities:

☐ easy access   ☐ back-in   ☐ pull-through
☐ water   ☐ pet friendly   ☐ laundry
☐ paved   ☐ sewer   ☐ electricity
☐ 15 amp   ☐ 30 amp   ☐ 50 amp
☐ shade   ☐ pool   ☐ restrooms
☐ store   ☐ picnic table   ☐ fire ring
☐ firewood   ☐ tv   ☐ wifi
☐ security   ☐ ice   ☐ cafe

Activities:

☐ fishing   ☐ hiking   ☐ canoeing
☐ lake   ☐ river   ☐ hot tub
☐ fitness   ☐ bike   ☐ boat
☐ shuffleboard ☐ pickleball   ☐ golf

Camped with:_____
_____
_____

Places visited:_____
_____
_____

Visit/do next time:_____
_____
_____

Most memorable event:

Most fun things:

Notes:

Drawing or favorite photo:

Campground: _____ **Dates:** _____

Location:_____

Travel to Campground: *Miles:* _____ *Time:* _____ *Cost:* _____

Weather :

☐ ☐ ☐ ☐ ☐ ☐

Campground Information

Name:_____

Address:_____

Phone:_____

Site#:_____ Site for next time:_____

Cost:_____ $ ☐ Day ☐Week ☐Month

GPS:_____

Rating: ★☆☆☆☆☆☆☆☆☆

Water pressure ★☆☆☆☆☆ Location ★☆☆☆☆

Cleanliness ★☆☆☆☆☆ Site size ★☆☆☆☆

Restrooms ★☆☆☆☆☆ Noise ★☆☆☆☆

Amenities:

☐ easy access ☐ back-in ☐ pull-through
☐ water ☐ pet friendly ☐ laundry
☐ paved ☐ sewer ☐ electricity
☐ 15 amp ☐ 30 amp ☐ 50 amp
☐ shade ☐ pool ☐ restrooms
☐ store ☐ picnic table ☐ fire ring
☐ firewood ☐ tv ☐ wifi
☐ security ☐ ice ☐ cafe

Activities:

☐ fishing ☐ hiking ☐ canoeing
☐ lake ☐ river ☐ hot tub
☐ fitness ☐ bike ☐ boat
☐ shuffleboard ☐ pickleball ☐ golf

Camped with:_____

_____

_____

Places visited:_____

_____

_____

Visit/do next time:_____

_____

_____

Most memorable event:

Most fun things:

Notes:

Drawing or favorite photo:

Campground: _____ Dates: _____

Location: _____

Travel to Campground: *Miles:* _____ *Time:* _____ *Cost:* _____

Weather : ☀️ ⛅ ☁️ 🌧️ ⛈️ ❄️
☐ ☐ ☐ ☐ ☐ ☐

Campground Information

Name: _____

Address: _____

Phone: _____

Site#: _____ Site for next time: _____

Cost: _____ $ ☐ Day ☐ Week ☐ Month

GPS: _____

Rating: ★☆☆☆☆☆☆☆☆☆

Water pressure ★☆☆☆☆ Location ★☆☆☆☆

Cleanliness ★☆☆☆☆ Site size ★☆☆☆☆

Restrooms ★☆☆☆☆ Noise ★☆☆☆☆

Amenities:

☐ easy access	☐ back-in	☐ pull-through
☐ water	☐ pet friendly	☐ laundry
☐ paved	☐ sewer	☐ electricity
☐ 15 amp	☐ 30 amp	☐ 50 amp
☐ shade	☐ pool	☐ restrooms
☐ store	☐ picnic table	☐ fire ring
☐ firewood	☐ tv	☐ wifi
☐ security	☐ ice	☐ cafe

Activities:

☐ fishing	☐ hiking	☐ canoeing
☐ lake	☐ river	☐ hot tub
☐ fitness	☐ bike	☐ boat
☐ shuffleboard	☐ pickleball	☐ golf

Camped with: _____

_____

Places visited: _____

_____

Visit/do next time: _____

_____

Most memorable event:

Most fun things:

Notes:

Drawing or favorite photo:

Campground: _____ **Dates:** _____

Location: _____

Travel to Campground: *Miles:* _____ *Time:* _____ *Cost:* _____

Weather : ☀️ ⛅ ☁️ 🌧️ ⛈️ ❄️
☐ ☐ ☐ ☐ ☐ ☐

Campground Information

Name: _____

Address: _____

Phone: _____

Site#: _____ Site for next time: _____

Cost: _____ $ ☐ Day ☐ Week ☐ Month

GPS: _____

Rating: ★☆☆☆☆☆☆☆☆☆

Water pressure ★☆☆☆☆ Location ★☆☆☆☆
Cleanliness ★☆☆☆☆ Site size ★☆☆☆☆
Restrooms ★☆☆☆☆ Noise ★☆☆☆☆

Amenities:

☐ easy access ☐ back-in ☐ pull-through
☐ water ☐ pet friendly ☐ laundry
☐ paved ☐ sewer ☐ electricity
☐ 15 amp ☐ 30 amp ☐ 50 amp
☐ shade ☐ pool ☐ restrooms
☐ store ☐ picnic table ☐ fire ring
☐ firewood ☐ tv ☐ wifi
☐ security ☐ ice ☐ cafe

Activities:

☐ fishing ☐ hiking ☐ canoeing
☐ lake ☐ river ☐ hot tub
☐ fitness ☐ bike ☐ boat
☐ shuffleboard ☐ pickleball ☐ golf

Camped with: _____

_____

Places visited: _____

_____

Visit/do next time: _____

_____

Most memorable event:_____

_____

Most fun things:_____

_____

_____

Notes:_____

_____

_____

_____

_____

Drawing or favorite photo:

Campground: Dates:

Location:_____

Travel to Campground: *Miles:* _____ *Time:* _____ *Cost:* _____

Weather : ☀️ 🌤️ ☁️ 🌧️ ⛈️ ❄️
☐ ☐ ☐ ☐ ☐ ☐

Campground Information

Name:_____

Address:_____

Phone:_____

Site#:_____ Site for next time:_____

Cost:_____ $ ☐ Day ☐ Week ☐ Month

GPS:_____

Rating: ★☆☆☆☆☆☆☆☆☆

Water pressure ★☆☆☆☆☆ **Location** ★☆☆☆☆☆

Cleanliness ★☆☆☆☆☆ **Site size** ★☆☆☆☆☆

Restrooms ★☆☆☆☆☆ **Noise** ★☆☆☆☆☆

Amenities:

☐ easy access   ☐ back-in   ☐ pull-through
☐ water   ☐ pet friendly   ☐ laundry
☐ paved   ☐ sewer   ☐ electricity
☐ 15 amp   ☐ 30 amp   ☐ 50 amp
☐ shade   ☐ pool   ☐ restrooms
☐ store   ☐ picnic table   ☐ fire ring
☐ firewood   ☐ tv   ☐ wifi
☐ security   ☐ ice   ☐ cafe

Activities:

☐ fishing   ☐ hiking   ☐ canoeing
☐ lake   ☐ river   ☐ hot tub
☐ fitness   ☐ bike   ☐ boat
☐ shuffleboard   ☐ pickleball   ☐ golf

Camped with:_____

_____

_____

Places visited:_____

_____

_____

Visit/do next time:_____

_____

_____

Most memorable event:

Most fun things:

Notes:

Drawing or favorite photo:

Campground: Dates:

Location:_____

Travel to Campground: *Miles:*_____ *Time:*_____ *Cost:*_____

Weather : ☐ ☐ ☐ ☐ ☐ ☐

Campground Information

Name:_____

Address:_____

Phone:_____

Site#:_____ Site for next time:_____

Cost:_____ $ ☐ Day ☐ Week ☐ Month

GPS:_____

Rating: ★☆☆☆☆☆☆☆☆☆

Water pressure ★☆☆☆☆ Location ★☆☆☆☆

Cleanliness ★☆☆☆☆ Site size ★☆☆☆☆

Restrooms ★☆☆☆☆ Noise ★☆☆☆☆

Amenities:

☐ easy access ☐ back-in ☐ pull-through
☐ water ☐ pet friendly ☐ laundry
☐ paved ☐ sewer ☐ electricity
☐ 15 amp ☐ 30 amp ☐ 50 amp
☐ shade ☐ pool ☐ restrooms
☐ store ☐ picnic table ☐ fire ring
☐ firewood ☐ tv ☐ wifi
☐ security ☐ ice ☐ cafe

Activities:

☐ fishing ☐ hiking ☐ canoeing
☐ lake ☐ river ☐ hot tub
☐ fitness ☐ bike ☐ boat
☐ shuffleboard ☐ pickleball ☐ golf

Camped with:_____

_____

_____

Places visited:_____

_____

_____

Visit/do next time:_____

_____

_____

Most memorable event:

_____

_____

Most fun things:

_____

_____

_____

Notes:

_____

_____

_____

_____

_____

Drawing or favorite photo:

Campground: _____ **Dates:** _____

Location: _____

Travel to Campground: *Miles:* _____ *Time:* _____ *Cost:* _____

Weather : ☀️ ⛅ ☁️ 🌧️ ⛈️ ❄️
⬜ ⬜ ⬜ ⬜ ⬜ ⬜

Campground Information

Name: _____

Address: _____

Phone: _____

Site#: _____ Site for next time: _____

Cost: _____ $ ⬜ Day ⬜Week ⬜Month

GPS: _____

Rating: ⭐☆☆☆☆☆☆☆☆☆

Water pressure ⭐☆☆☆☆ Location ⭐☆☆☆☆

Cleanliness ⭐☆☆☆☆ Site size ⭐☆☆☆☆

Restrooms ⭐☆☆☆☆ Noise ⭐☆☆☆☆

Amenities:

⬜ easy access ⬜ back-in ⬜ pull-through
⬜ water ⬜ pet friendly ⬜ laundry
⬜ paved ⬜ sewer ⬜ electricity
⬜ 15 amp ⬜ 30 amp ⬜ 50 amp
⬜ shade ⬜ pool ⬜ restrooms
⬜ store ⬜ picnic table ⬜ fire ring
⬜ firewood ⬜ tv ⬜ wifi
⬜ security ⬜ ice ⬜ cafe

Activities:

⬜ fishing ⬜ hiking ⬜ canoeing
⬜ lake ⬜ river ⬜ hot tub
⬜ fitness ⬜ bike ⬜ boat
⬜ shuffleboard ⬜ pickleball ⬜ golf

Camped with: _____

_____

_____

Places visited: _____

_____

_____

Visit/do next time: _____

_____

_____

Most memorable event:_____

_____

_____

Most fun things:_____

_____

_____

_____

Notes:_____

_____

_____

_____

_____

Drawing or favorite photo:

Campground: _____ Dates: _____

Location: _____

Travel to Campground: *Miles:* _____ *Time:* _____ *Cost:* _____

Weather : ☐ ☐ ☐ ☐ ☐ ☐

Campground Information

Name: _____

Address: _____

Phone: _____

Site#: _____ Site for next time: _____

Cost: _____ $ ☐ Day ☐Week ☐Month

GPS: _____

Rating: ★☆☆☆☆☆☆☆☆☆

Water pressure ★☆☆☆☆ Location ★☆☆☆☆

Cleanliness ★☆☆☆☆ Site size ★☆☆☆☆

Restrooms ★☆☆☆☆ Noise ★☆☆☆☆

Amenities:

☐ easy access   ☐ back-in   ☐ pull-through
☐ water   ☐ pet friendly   ☐ laundry
☐ paved   ☐ sewer   ☐ electricity
☐ 15 amp   ☐ 30 amp   ☐ 50 amp
☐ shade   ☐ pool   ☐ restrooms
☐ store   ☐ picnic table   ☐ fire ring
☐ firewood   ☐ tv   ☐ wifi
☐ security   ☐ ice   ☐ cafe

Activities:

☐ fishing   ☐ hiking   ☐ canoeing
☐ lake   ☐ river   ☐ hot tub
☐ fitness   ☐ bike   ☐ boat
☐ shuffleboard   ☐ pickleball   ☐ golf

Camped with: _____

_____

_____

Places visited: _____

_____

_____

Visit/do next time: _____

_____

_____

Most memorable event:

Most fun things:

Notes:

Drawing or favorite photo:

Campground: Dates:

Location:_____

Travel to Campground: *Miles:* _____ *Time:* _____ *Cost:* _____

Weather :   ☀️ ⬜   ⛅ ⬜   ☁️ ⬜   🌧️ ⬜   ⛈️ ⬜   ❄️ ⬜

Campground Information

Name:_____

Address:_____

Phone:_____

Site#:_____ Site for next time:_____

Cost:_____ $ ☐ Day ☐ Week ☐ Month

GPS:_____

Rating: ★☆☆☆☆☆☆☆☆☆

Water pressure ★☆☆☆☆☆ Location ★☆☆☆☆☆

Cleanliness ★☆☆☆☆☆ Site size ★☆☆☆☆☆

Restrooms ★☆☆☆☆☆ Noise ★☆☆☆☆☆

Amenities:

☐ easy access   ☐ back-in   ☐ pull-through
☐ water   ☐ pet friendly   ☐ laundry
☐ paved   ☐ sewer   ☐ electricity
☐ 15 amp   ☐ 30 amp   ☐ 50 amp
☐ shade   ☐ pool   ☐ restrooms
☐ store   ☐ picnic table   ☐ fire ring
☐ firewood   ☐ tv   ☐ wifi
☐ security   ☐ ice   ☐ cafe

Activities:

☐ fishing   ☐ hiking   ☐ canoeing
☐ lake   ☐ river   ☐ hot tub
☐ fitness   ☐ bike   ☐ boat
☐ shuffleboard ☐ pickleball   ☐ golf

Camped with:_____
_____
_____

Places visited:_____
_____
_____

Visit/do next time:_____
_____
_____

Most memorable event:

Most fun things:

Notes:

Drawing or favorite photo:

Campground: Dates:

Location:_____

Travel to Campground: *Miles:* _____ *Time:* _____ *Cost:* _____

Weather : ☀️ ⛅ ☁️ 🌧️ ⛈️ ❄️
◻️ ◻️ ◻️ ◻️ ◻️ ◻️

Campground Information

Name:_____

Address:_____

Phone:_____

Site#:_____ Site for next time:_____

Cost:_____ $ ◻️ Day ◻️Week ◻️Month

GPS:_____

Rating: ★☆☆☆☆☆☆☆☆☆

Water pressure ★☆☆☆☆☆ **Location** ★☆☆☆☆☆

Cleanliness ★☆☆☆☆☆ **Site size** ★☆☆☆☆☆

Restrooms ★☆☆☆☆☆ **Noise** ★☆☆☆☆☆

Amenities:

◻️ easy access   ◻️ back-in   ◻️ pull-through
◻️ water   ◻️ pet friendly ◻️ laundry
◻️ paved   ◻️ sewer   ◻️ electricity
◻️ 15 amp   ◻️ 30 amp   ◻️ 50 amp
◻️ shade   ◻️ pool   ◻️ restrooms
◻️ store   ◻️ picnic table ◻️ fire ring
◻️ firewood   ◻️ tv   ◻️ wifi
◻️ security   ◻️ ice   ◻️ cafe

Activities:

◻️ fishing   ◻️ hiking   ◻️ canoeing
◻️ lake   ◻️ river   ◻️ hot tub
◻️ fitness   ◻️ bike   ◻️ boat
◻️ shuffleboard   ◻️ pickleball   ◻️ golf

Camped with:_____
_____
_____

Places visited:_____
_____
_____

Visit/do next time:_____
_____
_____

Most memorable event:

Most fun things:

Notes:

Drawing or favorite photo:

Campground: _____ **Dates:** _____

Location:_____

Travel to Campground: *Miles:* _____ *Time:* _____ *Cost:* _____

Weather : ☀️ ⛅ ☁️ 🌧️ ⛈️ ❄️
⬜ ⬜ ⬜ ⬜ ⬜ ⬜

Campground Information

Name:_____

Address:_____

Phone:_____

Site#:_____ Site for next time:_____

Cost:_____ $ ☐ Day ☐Week ☐Month

GPS:_____

Rating: ★☆☆☆☆☆☆☆☆☆

Water pressure ★☆☆☆☆ Location ★☆☆☆☆

Cleanliness ★☆☆☆☆ Site size ★☆☆☆☆

Restrooms ★☆☆☆☆ Noise ★☆☆☆☆

Amenities:

☐ easy access ☐ back-in ☐ pull-through
☐ water ☐ pet friendly ☐ laundry
☐ paved ☐ sewer ☐ electricity
☐ 15 amp ☐ 30 amp ☐ 50 amp
☐ shade ☐ pool ☐ restrooms
☐ store ☐ picnic table ☐ fire ring
☐ firewood ☐ tv ☐ wifi
☐ security ☐ ice ☐ cafe

Activities:

☐ fishing ☐ hiking ☐ canoeing
☐ lake ☐ river ☐ hot tub
☐ fitness ☐ bike ☐ boat
☐ shuffleboard ☐ pickleball ☐ golf

Camped with:_____

_____

Places visited:_____

_____

Visit/do next time:_____

_____

Most memorable event:_____

_____

Most fun things:_____

_____

_____

Notes:_____

_____

_____

_____

Drawing or favorite photo:

Campground: Dates:

Location:_____

Travel to Campground: *Miles:* _____ *Time:* _____ *Cost:* _____

Weather : ☐ ☐ ☐ ☐ ☐ ☐

Campground Information

Name:_____

Address:_____

Phone:_____

Site#:_____ Site for next time:_____

Cost:_____ $ ☐ Day ☐Week ☐Month

GPS:_____

Rating: ★☆☆☆☆☆☆☆☆☆

Water pressure ★☆☆☆☆ Location ★☆☆☆☆

Cleanliness ★☆☆☆☆ Site size ★☆☆☆☆

Restrooms ★☆☆☆☆ Noise ★☆☆☆☆

Amenities:

☐ easy access ☐ back-in ☐ pull-through
☐ water ☐ pet friendly ☐ laundry
☐ paved ☐ sewer ☐ electricity
☐ 15 amp ☐ 30 amp ☐ 50 amp
☐ shade ☐ pool ☐ restrooms
☐ store ☐ picnic table ☐ fire ring
☐ firewood ☐ tv ☐ wifi
☐ security ☐ ice ☐ cafe

Activities:

☐ fishing ☐ hiking ☐ canoeing
☐ lake ☐ river ☐ hot tub
☐ fitness ☐ bike ☐ boat
☐ shuffleboard ☐ pickleball ☐ golf

Camped with:_____

_____

Places visited:_____

_____

Visit/do next time:_____

_____

Most memorable event:

Most fun things:

Notes:

Drawing or favorite photo:

Campground:	Dates:

Location:_____

Travel to Campground: *Miles:* _____ *Time:* _____ *Cost:* _____

Weather :

☐ ☐ ☐ ☐ ☐ ☐

Campground Information

Name:_____

Address:_____

Phone:_____

Site#:_____ Site for next time:_____

Cost:_____ $ ☐ Day ☐Week ☐Month

GPS:_____

Rating: ★☆☆☆☆☆☆☆☆☆

Water pressure ★☆☆☆☆ **Location** ★☆☆☆☆

Cleanliness ★☆☆☆☆ **Site size** ★☆☆☆☆

Restrooms ★☆☆☆☆ **Noise** ★☆☆☆☆

Amenities:

☐ easy access ☐ back-in ☐ pull-through
☐ water ☐ pet friendly ☐ laundry
☐ paved ☐ sewer ☐ electricity
☐ 15 amp ☐ 30 amp ☐ 50 amp
☐ shade ☐ pool ☐ restrooms
☐ store ☐ picnic table ☐ fire ring
☐ firewood ☐ tv ☐ wifi
☐ security ☐ ice ☐ cafe

Activities:

☐ fishing ☐ hiking ☐ canoeing
☐ lake ☐ river ☐ hot tub
☐ fitness ☐ bike ☐ boat
☐ shuffleboard ☐ pickleball ☐ golf

Camped with:_____

_____

_____

Places visited:_____

_____

_____

Visit/do next time:_____

_____

_____

Most memorable event:

Most fun things:

Notes:

Drawing or favorite photo:

Campground: _____ **Dates:** _____

Location: _____

Travel to Campground: *Miles:* _____ *Time:* _____ *Cost:* _____

Weather : ☐ ☐ ☐ ☐ ☐ ☐

Campground Information

Name: _____

Address: _____

Phone: _____

Site#: _____ **Site for next time:** _____

Cost: _____ $ ☐ Day ☐ Week ☐ Month

GPS: _____

Rating: ★☆☆☆☆☆☆☆☆☆

Water pressure ★☆☆☆☆ **Location** ★☆☆☆☆

Cleanliness ★☆☆☆☆ **Site size** ★☆☆☆☆

Restrooms ★☆☆☆☆ **Noise** ★☆☆☆☆

Amenities:

☐ easy access ☐ back-in ☐ pull-through
☐ water ☐ pet friendly ☐ laundry
☐ paved ☐ sewer ☐ electricity
☐ 15 amp ☐ 30 amp ☐ 50 amp
☐ shade ☐ pool ☐ restrooms
☐ store ☐ picnic table ☐ fire ring
☐ firewood ☐ tv ☐ wifi
☐ security ☐ ice ☐ cafe

Activities:

☐ fishing ☐ hiking ☐ canoeing
☐ lake ☐ river ☐ hot tub
☐ fitness ☐ bike ☐ boat
☐ shuffleboard ☐ pickleball ☐ golf

Camped with: _____

_____

_____

Places visited: _____

_____

_____

Visit/do next time: _____

_____

_____

Most memorable event:

_____

_____

Most fun things:

_____

_____

_____

Notes:

_____

_____

_____

_____

_____

Drawing or favorite photo:

Campground: _____ **Dates:** _____

Location:_____

Travel to Campground: *Miles:* _____ *Time:* _____ *Cost:* _____

Weather : ☀️ ⛅ ☁️ 🌧️ ⛈️ ❄️
⬜ ⬜ ⬜ ⬜ ⬜ ⬜

Campground Information

Name:_____

Address:_____

Phone:_____

Site#:_____ Site for next time:_____

Cost:_____ $ ☐ Day ☐Week ☐Month

GPS:_____

Rating: ★☆☆☆☆☆☆☆☆☆

Water pressure ★☆☆☆☆☆ Location ★☆☆☆☆☆

Cleanliness ★☆☆☆☆☆ Site size ★☆☆☆☆☆

Restrooms ★☆☆☆☆☆ Noise ★☆☆☆☆☆

Amenities:

☐ easy access ☐ back-in ☐ pull-through
☐ water ☐ pet friendly ☐ laundry
☐ paved ☐ sewer ☐ electricity
☐ 15 amp ☐ 30 amp ☐ 50 amp
☐ shade ☐ pool ☐ restrooms
☐ store ☐ picnic table ☐ fire ring
☐ firewood ☐ tv ☐ wifi
☐ security ☐ ice ☐ cafe

Activities:

☐ fishing ☐ hiking ☐ canoeing
☐ lake ☐ river ☐ hot tub
☐ fitness ☐ bike ☐ boat
☐ shuffleboard ☐ pickleball ☐ golf

Camped with:_____

_____

_____

Places visited:_____

_____

_____

Visit/do next time:_____

_____

_____

Most memorable event:

_____

_____

Most fun things:

_____

_____

_____

Notes:

_____

_____

_____

_____

Drawing or favorite photo:

Campground: Dates:

Location:_____

Travel to Campground: *Miles:* _____ *Time:* _____ *Cost:* _____

Weather : ☀ ⛅ ☁ 🌧 ⛈ ❄
☐ ☐ ☐ ☐ ☐ ☐

Campground Information

Name:_____

Address:_____

Phone:_____

Site#:_____ Site for next time:_____

Cost:_____ $ ☐ Day ☐Week ☐Month

GPS:_____

Rating: ★☆☆☆☆☆☆☆☆☆

Water pressure ★☆☆☆☆ **Location** ★☆☆☆☆

Cleanliness ★☆☆☆☆ **Site size** ★☆☆☆☆

Restrooms ★☆☆☆☆ **Noise** ★☆☆☆☆

Amenities:

☐ easy access	☐ back-in	☐ pull-through
☐ water	☐ pet friendly	☐ laundry
☐ paved	☐ sewer	☐ electricity
☐ 15 amp	☐ 30 amp	☐ 50 amp
☐ shade	☐ pool	☐ restrooms
☐ store	☐ picnic table	☐ fire ring
☐ firewood	☐ tv	☐ wifi
☐ security	☐ ice	☐ cafe

Activities:

☐ fishing	☐ hiking	☐ canoeing
☐ lake	☐ river	☐ hot tub
☐ fitness	☐ bike	☐ boat
☐ shuffleboard	☐ pickleball	☐ golf

Camped with:_____

_____

Places visited:_____

_____

Visit/do next time:_____

_____

Most memorable event:_____
_____

Most fun things:_____
_____
_____

Notes:_____
_____
_____
_____
_____

Drawing or favorite photo:

Campground: Dates:

Location:_____

Travel to Campground: *Miles:* _____ *Time:* _____ *Cost:* _____

Weather : ☀️ ⛅ ☁️ 🌧️ ⛈️ ❄️
☐ ☐ ☐ ☐ ☐ ☐

Campground Information

Name:_____

Address:_____

Phone:_____

Site#:_____ Site for next time:_____

Cost:_____ $ ☐ Day ☐Week ☐Month

GPS:_____

Rating: ★☆☆☆☆☆☆☆☆☆

Water pressure ★☆☆☆☆☆ Location ★☆☆☆☆☆

Cleanliness ★☆☆☆☆☆ Site size ★☆☆☆☆☆

Restrooms ★☆☆☆☆☆ Noise ★☆☆☆☆☆

Amenities:

☐ easy access	☐ back-in	☐ pull-through
☐ water	☐ pet friendly	☐ laundry
☐ paved	☐ sewer	☐ electricity
☐ 15 amp	☐ 30 amp	☐ 50 amp
☐ shade	☐ pool	☐ restrooms
☐ store	☐ picnic table	☐ fire ring
☐ firewood	☐ tv	☐ wifi
☐ security	☐ ice	☐ cafe

Activities:

☐ fishing	☐ hiking	☐ canoeing
☐ lake	☐ river	☐ hot tub
☐ fitness	☐ bike	☐ boat
☐ shuffleboard	☐ pickleball	☐ golf

Camped with:_____

_____

_____

Places visited:_____

_____

_____

Visit/do next time:_____

_____

_____

Most memorable event:

Most fun things:

Notes:

Drawing or favorite photo:

Campground: Dates:

Location:_____

Travel to Campground: *Miles:* _____ *Time:* _____ *Cost:* _____

Weather : ☀️ ⛅ ☁️ 🌧️ ⛈️ ❄️
☐   ☐   ☐   ☐   ☐   ☐

Campground Information

Name:_____

Address:_____

Phone:_____

Site#:_____ Site for next time:_____

Cost:_____ $ ☐ Day ☐ Week ☐ Month

GPS:_____

Rating: ★☆☆☆☆☆☆☆☆☆

Water pressure ★☆☆☆☆ Location ★☆☆☆☆

Cleanliness ★☆☆☆☆ Site size ★☆☆☆☆

Restrooms ★☆☆☆☆ Noise ★☆☆☆☆

Amenities:

☐ easy access ☐ back-in ☐ pull-through
☐ water ☐ pet friendly ☐ laundry
☐ paved ☐ sewer ☐ electricity
☐ 15 amp ☐ 30 amp ☐ 50 amp
☐ shade ☐ pool ☐ restrooms
☐ store ☐ picnic table ☐ fire ring
☐ firewood ☐ tv ☐ wifi
☐ security ☐ ice ☐ cafe

Activities:

☐ fishing ☐ hiking ☐ canoeing
☐ lake ☐ river ☐ hot tub
☐ fitness ☐ bike ☐ boat
☐ shuffleboard ☐ pickleball ☐ golf

Camped with:_____

_____

Places visited:_____

_____

Visit/do next time:_____

_____

Most memorable event:

_____

_____

Most fun things:

_____

_____

_____

Notes:

_____

_____

_____

_____

_____

Drawing or favorite photo:

Campground: Dates:

Location:_____

Travel to Campground: *Miles:* _____ *Time:* _____ *Cost:* _____

Weather : ☀️ ☁️ ☁️ 🌧️ ⛈️ ❄️
       ☐   ☐   ☐   ☐   ☐   ☐

Campground Information

Name:_____

Address:_____

Phone:_____

Site#:_____ Site for next time:_____

Cost:_____ $ ☐ Day ☐Week ☐Month

GPS:_____

Rating: ★☆☆☆☆☆☆☆☆☆

Water pressure ★☆☆☆☆ Location ★☆☆☆☆

Cleanliness ★☆☆☆☆ Site size ★☆☆☆☆

Restrooms ★☆☆☆☆ Noise ★☆☆☆☆

Amenities:

☐ easy access   ☐ back-in   ☐ pull-through
☐ water   ☐ pet friendly   ☐ laundry
☐ paved   ☐ sewer   ☐ electricity
☐ 15 amp   ☐ 30 amp   ☐ 50 amp
☐ shade   ☐ pool   ☐ restrooms
☐ store   ☐ picnic table   ☐ fire ring
☐ firewood   ☐ tv   ☐ wifi
☐ security   ☐ ice   ☐ cafe

Activities:

☐ fishing   ☐ hiking   ☐ canoeing
☐ lake   ☐ river   ☐ hot tub
☐ fitness   ☐ bike   ☐ boat
☐ shuffleboard   ☐ pickleball   ☐ golf

Camped with:_____

_____

Places visited:_____

_____

Visit/do next time:_____

_____

Most memorable event:

Most fun things:

Notes:

Drawing or favorite photo:

Campground: _____ Dates: _____

Location: _____

Travel to Campground: *Miles:* _____ *Time:* _____ *Cost:* _____

Weather : ☀️ ⛅ ☁️ 🌧️ ⛈️ ❄️

☐ ☐ ☐ ☐ ☐ ☐

Campground Information

Name: _____

Address: _____

Phone: _____

Site#: _____ Site for next time: _____

Cost: _____ $ ☐ Day ☐ Week ☐ Month

GPS: _____

Rating: ★☆☆☆☆☆☆☆☆☆

Water pressure ★☆☆☆☆ Location ★☆☆☆☆

Cleanliness ★☆☆☆☆ Site size ★☆☆☆☆

Restrooms ★☆☆☆☆ Noise ★☆☆☆☆

Amenities:

☐ easy access ☐ back-in ☐ pull-through
☐ water ☐ pet friendly ☐ laundry
☐ paved ☐ sewer ☐ electricity
☐ 15 amp ☐ 30 amp ☐ 50 amp
☐ shade ☐ pool ☐ restrooms
☐ store ☐ picnic table ☐ fire ring
☐ firewood ☐ tv ☐ wifi
☐ security ☐ ice ☐ cafe

Activities:

☐ fishing ☐ hiking ☐ canoeing
☐ lake ☐ river ☐ hot tub
☐ fitness ☐ bike ☐ boat
☐ shuffleboard ☐ pickleball ☐ golf

Camped with: _____

_____

Places visited: _____

_____

Visit/do next time: _____

_____

Most memorable event:_____
_____

Most fun things:_____
_____
_____
_____

Notes:_____
_____
_____
_____
_____

Drawing or favorite photo:

Campground: Dates:

Location:_____

Travel to Campground: *Miles:*_____ *Time:*_____ *Cost:*_____

Weather : ☀️ 🌤️ ☁️ 🌧️ ⛈️ ❄️
⬜ ⬜ ⬜ ⬜ ⬜ ⬜

Campground Information

Name:_____

Address:_____

Phone:_____

Site#:_____ Site for next time:_____

Cost:_____ $ ☐ Day ☐Week ☐Month

GPS:_____

Rating: ★☆☆☆☆☆☆☆☆☆

Water pressure ★☆☆☆☆ Location ★☆☆☆☆

Cleanliness ★☆☆☆☆ Site size ★☆☆☆☆

Restrooms ★☆☆☆☆ Noise ★☆☆☆☆

Amenities:

☐ easy access   ☐ back-in   ☐ pull-through
☐ water   ☐ pet friendly   ☐ laundry
☐ paved   ☐ sewer   ☐ electricity
☐ 15 amp   ☐ 30 amp   ☐ 50 amp
☐ shade   ☐ pool   ☐ restrooms
☐ store   ☐ picnic table   ☐ fire ring
☐ firewood   ☐ tv   ☐ wifi
☐ security   ☐ ice   ☐ cafe

Activities:

☐ fishing   ☐ hiking   ☐ canoeing
☐ lake   ☐ river   ☐ hot tub
☐ fitness   ☐ bike   ☐ boat
☐ shuffleboard   ☐ pickleball   ☐ golf

Camped with:_____

_____

_____

Places visited:_____

_____

_____

Visit/do next time:_____

_____

_____

Most memorable event:

Most fun things:

Notes:

Drawing or favorite photo:

Campground:	Dates:

Location:_____

Travel to Campground: *Miles:*_____ *Time:*_____ *Cost:*_____

Weather : ☀ ⛅ ☁ 🌧 ⛈ ❄
⬜ ⬜ ⬜ ⬜ ⬜ ⬜

Campground Information

Name:_____

Address:_____

Phone:_____

Site#:_____ Site for next time:_____

Cost:_____ $ ☐ Day ☐Week ☐Month

GPS:_____

Rating: ★☆☆☆☆☆☆☆☆☆

Water pressure ★☆☆☆☆ Location ★☆☆☆☆

Cleanliness ★☆☆☆☆ Site size ★☆☆☆☆

Restrooms ★☆☆☆☆ Noise ★☆☆☆☆

Amenities:

☐ easy access ☐ back-in ☐ pull-through
☐ water ☐ pet friendly ☐ laundry
☐ paved ☐ sewer ☐ electricity
☐ 15 amp ☐ 30 amp ☐ 50 amp
☐ shade ☐ pool ☐ restrooms
☐ store ☐ picnic table ☐ fire ring
☐ firewood ☐ tv ☐ wifi
☐ security ☐ ice ☐ cafe

Activities:

☐ fishing ☐ hiking ☐ canoeing
☐ lake ☐ river ☐ hot tub
☐ fitness ☐ bike ☐ boat
☐ shuffleboard ☐ pickleball ☐ golf

Camped with:_____
_____
_____

Places visited:_____
_____
_____

Visit/do next time:_____
_____
_____

Most memorable event:_____

_____

Most fun things:_____

_____

_____

_____

Notes:_____

_____

_____

_____

_____

Drawing or favorite photo:

Campground: _____ Dates: _____

Location: _____

Travel to Campground: *Miles:* _____ *Time:* _____ *Cost:* _____

Weather : ☼ ☐ ⛅ ☐ ☁ ☐ 🌧 ☐ ⛈ ☐ ❄ ☐

Campground Information

Name: _____

Address: _____

Phone: _____

Site#: _____ Site for next time: _____

Cost: _____ $ ☐ Day ☐ Week ☐ Month

GPS: _____

Rating: ★☆☆☆☆☆☆☆☆☆

Water pressure ★☆☆☆☆ Location ★☆☆☆☆

Cleanliness ★☆☆☆☆ Site size ★☆☆☆☆

Restrooms ★☆☆☆☆ Noise ★☆☆☆☆

Amenities:

☐ easy access	☐ back-in	☐ pull-through
☐ water	☐ pet friendly	☐ laundry
☐ paved	☐ sewer	☐ electricity
☐ 15 amp	☐ 30 amp	☐ 50 amp
☐ shade	☐ pool	☐ restrooms
☐ store	☐ picnic table	☐ fire ring
☐ firewood	☐ tv	☐ wifi
☐ security	☐ ice	☐ cafe

Activities:

☐ fishing	☐ hiking	☐ canoeing
☐ lake	☐ river	☐ hot tub
☐ fitness	☐ bike	☐ boat
☐ shuffleboard	☐ pickleball	☐ golf

Camped with: _____

_____

_____

Places visited: _____

_____

_____

Visit/do next time: _____

_____

_____

Most memorable event:

_____

_____

Most fun things:

_____

_____

_____

Notes:

_____

_____

_____

_____

Drawing or favorite photo:

Campground: Dates:

Location:_____

Travel to Campground: *Miles:* _____ *Time:* _____ *Cost:* _____

Weather : ☀️ ⛅ ☁️ 🌧️ ⛈️ ❄️
☐ ☐ ☐ ☐ ☐ ☐

Campground Information

Name:_____

Address:_____

Phone:_____

Site#:_____ Site for next time:_____

Cost:_____ $ ☐ Day ☐ Week ☐ Month

GPS:_____

Rating: ★☆☆☆☆☆☆☆☆☆

Water pressure ★☆☆☆☆ Location ★☆☆☆☆

Cleanliness ★☆☆☆☆ Site size ★☆☆☆☆

Restrooms ★☆☆☆☆ Noise ★☆☆☆☆

Amenities:

☐ easy access	☐ back-in	☐ pull-through
☐ water	☐ pet friendly	☐ laundry
☐ paved	☐ sewer	☐ electricity
☐ 15 amp	☐ 30 amp	☐ 50 amp
☐ shade	☐ pool	☐ restrooms
☐ store	☐ picnic table	☐ fire ring
☐ firewood	☐ tv	☐ wifi
☐ security	☐ ice	☐ cafe

Activities:

☐ fishing	☐ hiking	☐ canoeing
☐ lake	☐ river	☐ hot tub
☐ fitness	☐ bike	☐ boat
☐ shuffleboard	☐ pickleball	☐ golf

Camped with:_____

_____

Places visited:_____

_____

Visit/do next time:_____

_____

Most memorable event:_____
_____

Most fun things:_____
_____
_____

Notes:_____
_____
_____
_____
_____

Drawing or favorite photo:

Campground: Dates:

Location:_____

Travel to Campground: *Miles:* _____ *Time:* _____ *Cost:* _____

Weather : ☀ ⛅ ☁ 🌧 ⛈ ❄
☐ ☐ ☐ ☐ ☐ ☐

Campground Information

Name:_____

Address:_____

Phone:_____

Site#:_____ Site for next time:_____

Cost:_____ $ ☐ Day ☐Week ☐Month

GPS:_____

Rating: ★☆☆☆☆☆☆☆☆☆

Water pressure ★☆☆☆☆ Location ★☆☆☆☆

Cleanliness ★☆☆☆☆ Site size ★☆☆☆☆

Restrooms ★☆☆☆☆ Noise ★☆☆☆☆

Amenities:

☐ easy access ☐ back-in ☐ pull-through
☐ water ☐ pet friendly ☐ laundry
☐ paved ☐ sewer ☐ electricity
☐ 15 amp ☐ 30 amp ☐ 50 amp
☐ shade ☐ pool ☐ restrooms
☐ store ☐ picnic table ☐ fire ring
☐ firewood ☐ tv ☐ wifi
☐ security ☐ ice ☐ cafe

Activities:

☐ fishing ☐ hiking ☐ canoeing
☐ lake ☐ river ☐ hot tub
☐ fitness ☐ bike ☐ boat
☐ shuffleboard ☐ pickleball ☐ golf

Camped with:_____

_____

_____

Places visited:_____

_____

_____

Visit/do next time:_____

_____

_____

Most memorable event:

Most fun things:

Notes:

Drawing or favorite photo:

Campground: Dates:

Location:_____

Travel to Campground: *Miles:* _____ *Time:* _____ *Cost:* _____

Weather : ☐ ☐ ☐ ☐ ☐ ☐

Campground Information

Name:_____

Address:_____

Phone:_____

Site#:_____ Site for next time:_____

Cost:_____ $ ☐ Day ☐ Week ☐ Month

GPS:_____

Rating: ★☆☆☆☆☆☆☆☆☆

Water pressure ★☆☆☆☆ Location ★☆☆☆☆

Cleanliness ★☆☆☆☆ Site size ★☆☆☆☆

Restrooms ★☆☆☆☆ Noise ★☆☆☆☆

Amenities:

☐ easy access ☐ back-in   ☐ pull-through
☐ water   ☐ pet friendly ☐ laundry
☐ paved   ☐ sewer   ☐ electricity
☐ 15 amp   ☐ 30 amp   ☐ 50 amp
☐ shade   ☐ pool   ☐ restrooms
☐ store   ☐ picnic table ☐ fire ring
☐ firewood   ☐ tv   ☐ wifi
☐ security   ☐ ice   ☐ cafe

Activities:

☐ fishing   ☐ hiking   ☐ canoeing
☐ lake   ☐ river   ☐ hot tub
☐ fitness   ☐ bike   ☐ boat
☐ shuffleboard ☐ pickleball   ☐ golf

Camped with:_____

_____

Places visited:_____

_____

Visit/do next time:_____

_____

Most memorable event:

_____

_____

Most fun things:

_____

_____

_____

Notes:

_____

_____

_____

_____

_____

Drawing or favorite photo:

Campground: Dates:

Location:_____

Travel to Campground: *Miles:* _____ *Time:* _____ *Cost:* _____

Weather : ☀️ ☐ ⛅ ☐ ☁️ ☐ 🌧️ ☐ ⛈️ ☐ ❄️ ☐

Campground Information

Name:_____

Address:_____

Phone:_____

Site#:_____ Site for next time:_____

Cost:_____ $ ☐ Day ☐ Week ☐ Month

GPS:_____

Rating: ⭐☆☆☆☆☆☆☆☆☆

Water pressure ⭐☆☆☆☆ **Location** ⭐☆☆☆☆

Cleanliness ⭐☆☆☆☆☆ **Site size** ⭐☆☆☆☆

Restrooms ⭐☆☆☆☆☆ **Noise** ⭐☆☆☆☆

Amenities:

☐ easy access ☐ back-in ☐ pull-through
☐ water ☐ pet friendly ☐ laundry
☐ paved ☐ sewer ☐ electricity
☐ 15 amp ☐ 30 amp ☐ 50 amp
☐ shade ☐ pool ☐ restrooms
☐ store ☐ picnic table ☐ fire ring
☐ firewood ☐ tv ☐ wifi
☐ security ☐ ice ☐ cafe

Activities:

☐ fishing ☐ hiking ☐ canoeing
☐ lake ☐ river ☐ hot tub
☐ fitness ☐ bike ☐ boat
☐ shuffleboard ☐ pickleball ☐ golf

Camped with:_____

_____

Places visited:_____

_____

Visit/do next time:_____

_____

Most memorable event:

Most fun things:

Notes:

Drawing or favorite photo:

Campground: _____ Dates: _____

Location:_____

Travel to Campground: *Miles:* _____ *Time:* _____ *Cost:* _____

Weather : ☀️ ⛅ ☁️ 🌧️ ⛈️ ❄️
⬜ ⬜ ⬜ ⬜ ⬜ ⬜

Campground Information

Name:_____

Address:_____

Phone:_____

Site#:_____ Site for next time:_____

Cost:_____ $ ☐ Day ☐Week ☐Month

GPS:_____

Rating: ★☆☆☆☆☆☆☆☆☆

Water pressure ★☆☆☆☆ Location ★☆☆☆☆

Cleanliness ★☆☆☆☆ Site size ★☆☆☆☆

Restrooms ★☆☆☆☆ Noise ★☆☆☆☆

Amenities:

☐ easy access ☐ back-in ☐ pull-through
☐ water ☐ pet friendly ☐ laundry
☐ paved ☐ sewer ☐ electricity
☐ 15 amp ☐ 30 amp ☐ 50 amp
☐ shade ☐ pool ☐ restrooms
☐ store ☐ picnic table ☐ fire ring
☐ firewood ☐ tv ☐ wifi
☐ security ☐ ice ☐ cafe

Activities:

☐ fishing ☐ hiking ☐ canoeing
☐ lake ☐ river ☐ hot tub
☐ fitness ☐ bike ☐ boat
☐ shuffleboard ☐ pickleball ☐ golf

Camped with:_____

_____

Places visited:_____

_____

Visit/do next time:_____

_____

Most memorable event:

_____

_____

Most fun things:

_____

_____

_____

Notes:

_____

_____

_____

_____

_____

Drawing or favorite photo:

Campground: **Dates:**

Location:_____

Travel to Campground: *Miles:*_____ *Time:*_____ *Cost:*_____

Weather : ☐ ☐ ☐ ☐ ☐ ☐

Campground Information

Name:_____

Address:_____

Phone:_____

Site#:_____ Site for next time:_____

Cost:_____ $ ☐ Day ☐ Week ☐ Month

GPS:_____

Rating: ★☆☆☆☆☆☆☆☆☆

Water pressure ★☆☆☆☆☆ Location ★☆☆☆☆☆

Cleanliness ★☆☆☆☆☆ Site size ★☆☆☆☆☆

Restrooms ★☆☆☆☆☆ Noise ★☆☆☆☆☆

Amenities:

☐ easy access   ☐ back-in   ☐ pull-through
☐ water   ☐ pet friendly   ☐ laundry
☐ paved   ☐ sewer   ☐ electricity
☐ 15 amp   ☐ 30 amp   ☐ 50 amp
☐ shade   ☐ pool   ☐ restrooms
☐ store   ☐ picnic table   ☐ fire ring
☐ firewood   ☐ tv   ☐ wifi
☐ security   ☐ ice   ☐ cafe

Activities:

☐ fishing   ☐ hiking   ☐ canoeing
☐ lake   ☐ river   ☐ hot tub
☐ fitness   ☐ bike   ☐ boat
☐ shuffleboard   ☐ pickleball   ☐ golf

Camped with:_____

_____

Places visited:_____

_____

Visit/do next time:_____

_____

Most memorable event:_____

_____

Most fun things:_____

_____

_____

Notes:_____

_____

_____

_____

_____

Drawing or favorite photo:

Campground: Dates:

Location:_____

Travel to Campground: *Miles:* _____ *Time:* _____ *Cost:* _____

Weather : ☐ ☐ ☐ ☐ ☐ ☐

Campground Information

Name:_____

Address:_____

Phone:_____

Site#:_____ Site for next time:_____

Cost:_____ $ ☐ Day ☐ Week ☐ Month

GPS:_____

Rating: ★☆☆☆☆☆☆☆☆☆

Water pressure ★☆☆☆☆ Location ★☆☆☆☆

Cleanliness ★☆☆☆☆ Site size ★☆☆☆☆

Restrooms ★☆☆☆☆ Noise ★☆☆☆☆

Amenities:

☐ easy access ☐ back-in ☐ pull-through
☐ water ☐ pet friendly ☐ laundry
☐ paved ☐ sewer ☐ electricity
☐ 15 amp ☐ 30 amp ☐ 50 amp
☐ shade ☐ pool ☐ restrooms
☐ store ☐ picnic table ☐ fire ring
☐ firewood ☐ tv ☐ wifi
☐ security ☐ ice ☐ cafe

Activities:

☐ fishing ☐ hiking ☐ canoeing
☐ lake ☐ river ☐ hot tub
☐ fitness ☐ bike ☐ boat
☐ shuffleboard ☐ pickleball ☐ golf

Camped with:_____

_____

_____

Places visited:_____

_____

_____

Visit/do next time:_____

_____

_____

Most memorable event:

_____

_____

Most fun things:

_____

_____

_____

Notes:

_____

_____

_____

_____

_____

Drawing or favorite photo:

Printed in Great Britain
by Amazon